THE BEST OF WHITE EAGLE

White Eagle Books Currently in Print

THE BEST OF

White Eagle

A Compilation from White Eagle's Teaching
With illustrations by Bodel Rikys

WHITE EAGLE PUBLISHING TRUST

NEW LANDS : LISS : HAMPSHIRE : GU33 7HY
www.whiteaglepublishing.org

First Published June 2011
Second Edition June 2014

British Library Cataloguing in Publication Data
A catalogue record for this book
is available from the British Library

ISBN 978-0-85487-237-4

*In this book the marginal notes indicate the title of the book from
which an extract is taken. Please refer to the list opposite the title
page for a complete list, and note that all the White Eagle books may
be ordered from bookshops, from the addresses on the inside back
cover, and via the website www.whiteaglepublishing.org*

Set in Monotype Dante by the Publisher and
Printed in the UK by the Halstan Printing Group, Amersham

CONTENTS

WE ARE going to suggest to you our brethren that the vision on which you keep your gaze should be the six-pointed Star, the symbol of the spirit, symbol of the spirit of Christ. As you hold your vision steadily and firmly on that Star, you will find yourself being drawn up so that you see things on your earth from a higher vantage point. When you view things from the valley, you cannot see the beauty that surrounds you in clear perspective, but when you are drawn up by the Star to a higher level, you see the various conditions and problems of life quite differently. All humanity needs to follow the Star. It will never lead you astray, never misguide you.

BEAUTIFUL ROAD HOME

1. Seeking

THE KEY that unlocks the door to these heavenly mysteries lies not in the human mind, but in the heart.

*A*LL SEEK *the light, yet not before others is your light lit: not even disclosed to your nearest and dearest, but in the innermost sanctuary, with no veil between you and your real self.*

*W*HEN *your heart centre opens in love and kindness towards all creatures, it begins to grow and to expand, and can be seen by those with clear vision as a light radiating forth.*

TREASURES OF THE MASTER WITHIN

*A*S YOU *aspire towards God, as you endeavour to let the divine light within expand and grow so that all your thoughts are positive and good, so that all your aspirations are heavenward, you will set in motion vibrations of power. You will yourself become a vortex of spiritual light and power, and you will command—even unconsciously—all good. Your life will then take on a new aspect. You will first begin to feel a quiet harmony within, a certain confidence in God. To know God is to have faith that all things are working together for good in your life, that all things will work together for good in the world.*

WHITE EAGLE ON FESTIVALS AND CELEBRATIONS

The Best of White Eagle

A Search for God

SOME people feel closer to spirit, or to God, in a garden—or on the moors or the mountains. Some, if they spoke from heart's truth, would tell you that they felt nearer to God on a lonely sea. Others feel nearer to God when listening to beautiful music. Others have felt close to God when they gazed upon or painted a beautiful picture. A mother might tell you that she felt God most when she gave birth to her child, or when she looked into its eyes, in that indescribable spiritual rapport that means so much to a mother. Two friends come nearer to God in the love they feel for each other, spirit to spirit.

These feelings cannot be put into earthly language; it can only be a silent communion and an inner knowing of God. You may recognize God in man and woman, God in your companion. You see, when you can feel and know the light of spirit in your companion, you are actually seeing God.

This is the goal and the ideal human life all are seeking—this moment when you realize the Light in a blinding flash; when you become at-one with God and life, with God and others. This is an experience which comes to you while living in a physical body; and this coming face-to-face with God is finding truth. You do not recognize it as truth yet, but you have a feeling. Yes, feelings can sometimes be misleading, but there is one factor which can never mislead. That is the sight of your spirit. Do you know what we mean? Spiritual vision, the vision which can look out on life and see God in manifestation through form. This is the search that you all follow—a search for God.

FURTHER
STEPS
ON A
SPIRITUAL
PATH

SIMPLICITY should be the prayer of every aspirant; because only when the soul becomes truly humble can it be receptive to the guidance and love of the invisible brethren and the angelic messengers who wait under God's command to come to you and to all human beings. The key that unlocks the door to these heavenly mysteries lies not in the human mind but in the heart. Truth is simple, but because it is so simple it is hidden from powerful intellects, or those who play with words, yet it is revealed to the loving heart.

Do not mistake us. We do not suggest that men and women of learning cannot receive this heavenly blessing, guidance and inspiration. We refer to those who are arrogant mentally, those blinded by their arrogance and who have yet to undergo an initiation or experience which through pain or joy (pain and joy are but reflections of each other) brings humility.

Each soul must go through such experiences, perhaps many times, before understanding what it means to be humble. The greatest mind is ever the humble mind; you will find this in all elder and wise brethren. Humility is indeed the most important virtue if the soul is to attain any degree of understanding and experience of God. Through the experience of human life with all its pain and joy, the soul is quickened and enabled to see truth—which means of course that it can recognize its relationship with the Eternal Spirit.

The Best of White Eagle

The Secret is Stillness

W ITH Christ anything can be accomplished; the
mistake that so many people make is to depend on their own power. For the secret is to enter the
heart chamber, the inner self, the place of tranquillity
and stillness, and there pray; in other words, to stand
on one side and let the God-power work through the
medium of the body, mind and soul. Then there is
nothing that cannot be accomplished because whatever is done is to the glory of God. Any soul able to
commune with God is ready to manifest God.

A number of the Master's miracles were concerned with the healing of the blind. The blind
represents those who lack understanding of spiritual truth. While their souls yearn for love they
cannot feel it, they cannot give it. They are unaware of the invisible worlds of great beauty and
radiance about them, or that they themselves live
in a world which, rightly viewed, is a world of spiritual glory. What wonderful work it is to be able
to open the eyes of those who dwell in darkness
and show them that there is no death, and there
need never be separation even when their beloved
quits his or her physical body for another world!
This is the work of those who have passed the Water Initiation, those who have controlled their psychic forces and who are able to see into the other
worlds, those who can then convey their vision of
truth to their companions.

Many people waste time and energy trying to
convince others of the spirit world. There is no need
to convince anybody. The best work is to give forth

Seeking

that power which teaches the soul when it is once ready. It is all a question of the evolution of the person concerned. There is a time for these things. Once the individual has earned the right to know spiritual truth, the teacher will be forthcoming. Sometimes men and women become excited and long to meet a master in the flesh. They are usually disappointed. But when they have at last reached the point where they are able to recognize a master, then the master will manifest. They themselves will by then have created the necessary conditions in which to receive from the master the illumination, teaching, comfort and help they require, in readiness for the next step on the path. It is a great work to restore sight to the blind; or, in other words, to be able to illumine them through the power of the Christ spirit within.

It is not the speech, it is not only the thoughts; it is the inner self of the human being that can become so powerful and so Christlike that it conveys healing, teaching, blessing. The effect of this cannot be superficial and transient, for it comes from God within the soul and is therefore eternal and infinite. Within every soul dwells God, although there are many layers to be peeled off before the Christ light can shine forth. Those who are a little more advanced than others can indeed sometimes help their brethren in the casting off of some of these outer coverings.

What is Real

ONE day you will realize that you are surrounded not only by spirit worlds and beings, but by finer physical or semi-physical worlds inhabited by people similar to yourself. Mingling with you sometimes are spirits not of this world but from other planets. It is not unknown for spirits from other planets to speak through a sensitive human instrument. Men and women are set in their ideas, and cannot get away from a one-track mind. But beyond that one-track mind are so many wonderful things, a glorious life of which you know nothing.

You find life difficult and lonely, and you feel as though you are always toiling; your feet are heavy and the road along which you drive yourself grows very hard. But learn to open your vision and have courage to believe what you want to believe. So many have said to us, 'Oh White Eagle, I wish I could believe! Give me proof and I will believe!' My dear child, the proof you cry out for is within you! You want to be assured that you are an eternal being, and that your Creator is all love? You want to know that there is nothing to fear in death? You want to know that you can never be separated from those you love? The answer to every question lies within your own being. You want to be sure that in your meditations you are not deluding yourself; that you are not just imagining something which looks very nice but is really only wispy and fantastic. When you rise in consciousness in your meditations and aspirations to your Creator, you become aware of something that is adorable and lovely. Oh, the breath of the Infinite! The perfume of that breath! Oh, the joy of that life! Is it real or is it something which will disappear in the morning?

We answer that all that is holy, all that is pure *Seeking*

and sweet and lovely is of God, and it is real. That is your real state of life. Hearing this, you will say, 'Why then are we down here imprisoned in this heavy body? Why has the world fallen to its present state if human life aeons ago was so beautiful? If this world was ever a Garden of Eden, what has happened to it since? What have we done to bring about this terrible state of existence?' Yes, what have you done? What are you doing now? That is more to the point. Because if you lived every moment in the consciousness of your Creator, in the consciousness of the Son of God, the Christ, you would no longer be battened down in darkness; nor would you suffer. That love of God and of the spiritual life is creative and will create beauty and harmony in your body, in your life, and in your surroundings. It will give you a spiritual life that cannot be scarred or hurt, darkened or sullied by the illusory selfish existence.

You may look at life from your earthly level and see nothing but chaos. You say, 'What a muddle life is! What a terrible state the world is in!' Yet divine law operates only for good, brings beauty and harmony into manifestation at the lowest level, which is physical matter. While material life may appear chaotic, it is ever evolving. If you trace any work from its beginning, you will see that at first it goes through a period of chaos. For example, one sees confusion when a building is being constructed. When a painter begins, his canvas will be a baffling mixture of colour and unfinished form. Or you may see the overwritten pages of a book in preparation, and they will appear chaotic.

So in the course of spiritual and physical evolution, chaos may appear to reign, and those who do not know will say, 'Oh, men and women are so bad and there is much evil in the world!' We would give you a vision, not of confusion and evil, but of an infinite power working in perfect order, from the heights to the depths, from heaven above right down to the physical and through all humanity. We would show you a process in all life of changing darkness into light. Light creates life. And even in the very lowest form of life, light is working amid the darkness. Divine law, the law of God, is working on evil, the positive state working on the negative, in a process that is gradually producing the perfect God-conscious being.

'Man–woman made perfect': these simple words express the whole truth. The light comes from heaven and dwells in the darkness; it works on the darkness—that is, on evil—and slowly, by an exact law and with perfect precision, creates the perfect form, the perfect soul, the perfect manifestation of the Son of God.

All over the earth can be found relics of great sun temples, and scientists puzzle their brains to work out how the ancients could have carried monster stones weighing many tons and built temples of them. The ancients knew the power of sound and rhythm, they understood the power and put it into operation. In some instances, they built their temples of etheric matter and light; and with the passing of time and the closing-down of human spiritual powers they solidified into stone. If you go to Stonehenge at certain times and open your inner vision you will see great angels there, the ancient ones, great ones from other planets whose power is centred there. Do you not see that creation is not a phenomenon confined to earth, or any one planet? It is cosmic in scope and all parts of it are one: there is constant interchange and intercommunication. In past ages, God-beings have come to earth. And so, in time, when the Lord God thinks it is good, and the earth people are ready, beings from outer space will come again and be seen and recognized by humanity, and they will bring great happiness to earth people.

The time will surely come when scientists, through their discoveries in the realms of physical science, will be faced with the truth that there is a spiritual as well as a physical universe. And when humankind discovers the wisdom of studying spiritual science, humanity will enter the most wonderful, the most beauteous world, for in doing so all will quite plainly see the true way of life, and will naturally develop all the Godlike qualities that are within.

You may think this lies a long way in the future; but if humanity passes this present test, and we think it will, humankind will then advance on that path of spiritual unfoldment, on all the various rays of development—the ray of science, of philosophy, education, occultism, art, music, healing and so on—and the influence of the great ones at the head of all these rays will be directed in full power upon humankind.

The Best of White Eagle

Life begins from the centre, from spirit, and radiates in ever-increasing circles or cycles of life, growing ever more perfect.

Illumination

THE BEAM of light and beauty in the dark place of life is the surest, finest and best way to bring the human mind into harmony with the divine Spirit. Of what use is it to stand in a dark room and contemplate the darkness? No progress is made in that way; but if a lighted candle or lamp is brought into that room, it illumines and reveals all. So we hold fast to this point of view, concentrating on perfection in a world that seems to many to be full of darkness and suffering. But humanity must open its eyes to the vision glorious, before it can take one step forward on the path that will lead it eventually to that perfection.

Life goes on and on, ever evolving, ever unfolding. Never think that life is coming to an end. The decay you see, particularly in the autumn before the winter rest comes, is truly very lovely. Decaying things are in reality beautiful, because decay makes room for something new and more beautiful still. Remember, the leaves fall because the new life is pushing them off. Nature's decay is nature's rebirth, and with the decay of all physical things God makes new life. In order to have new things you must push the old away; the old has to withdraw or gradually be absorbed into the new. This applies to the members of humanity, as well as to nature. We hope you will try always to think in this way; even when you lose loved ones, remember that their physical form has dissolved into something new, not an unhappy state, but a new and glorious one.

In the beginning was the Word; and the Word was with

God. Before the coming of the world, the *thought* of God created that which was created. The thought of peace and goodwill that the angels and the teachers continually send through to the earth plane comes so insistently because the teachers, the planetary lords, are endeavouring to sound the creative 'Word' of peace and unity. We ourselves see no other condition on earth but peace. Men and women live as in a dark house, truly blacked out, and cannot see that which lies close—much less the prospect to come. Lift up the blinds of your soul—that is, attune yourselves in your daily thoughts and aspirations—so that the windows of your soul, the seven centres of the soul, may become quickened: so that the soul can look forth with a clear, unhampered vision, and see all around the process of birth, of construction, of growth.

Listen

WHITE
EAGLE ON
FESTIVALS
AND
CELEBRA-
TIONS

IF YOU could but give yourselves time to withdraw from the outer or material planes of life, and listen! When sitting at peace in your garden, or walking in the open places within your towns, or in quiet country lanes, give yourselves time to listen to the voice of love, which will then surely make itself known in the quiet of your soul.

This, beloved brethren, is the great secret of life on the earth plane. Those who live on the material plane only are barren, are starved; whatever work they put their hand to do, if they are not contacting the spirit, or the voice of God, in the quiet of their own souls, they do not dwell in the fullness they were intended to by our Father–Mother. God has given unto His–Her children the gift of love, the gift of wisdom, which lies in the heart. Another name for this gift is the spirit of Christ.

Test our words for yourselves; observe those who are trying, according to their own understanding, to express artistic, musical or literary gifts, or the gift of healing, and note how many of these are in touch with that mysterious spiritual life. Those so in touch express the life of the spirit in their work; others working purely on the intellectual plane may give brilliant service, brilliant work to the world, but there is something lacking if the spirit does not shine through.

In a perfectly-executed piece of music—technically perfect—unless the spirit is within, it fails in its purpose. So cultivate the art of listening, in your quiet moments, to the spirit, and it will speak ever in one language, that of love. Love brings to your heart peace, kindliness, tolerance, a desire to forget selfish aims, and a longing to give that which your spirit has revealed to you, to the rest of humanity.

Service

YOU ASK us, 'White Eagle, what can we do to help humankind? And we answer:

By daily, hourly, every moment of your life endeavouring to realize your true self, which lies buried deep in your innermost being. It will rise in you like a stream of light on which you will be able to rise to a higher level of consciousness where you will find yourself enveloped in the power and love of God.

Practise this daily realization of the Great White Light within your own being and project it forth into the outer world. Then, my friends, the mists around the earth will be dispelled. Do not look to others to do the work for you. Everyone is their own saviour; and everyone is the saviour of all humankind.

Apply spiritual light and truth and love to your every action. Pray that the will of God may become manifest through you and in your life.

Let your brotherhood be not merely lip-service but brotherhood active and heartfelt in the smallest detail. You will have no need to worry then about the events which lie ahead. You can meet them with confidence and hope. You can be certain that you, a unit, are helping all humankind, for as part of the whole you can raise all people to receive succour from God.

The love of the Brotherhood is ever with you. Look to the light of the Star: it will never fail you.

THE aspirant today is not concerned with the monastic or ascetic life of old. He or she is called to mingle with humanity; to mingle with and bring through, into the minds of those he or she meets, the light of the ages.

TREASURES OF THE MASTER WITHIN

The Best of White Eagle

2. Thought

KEEP your thoughts always fixed upon the good, the true and the beautiful God-life.

*A*LL WILL *be good and will come right if you centre your vision upon God, because God is ever evolving, creating, bringing good out of evil, order out of chaos, light out of darkness.*

SPIRITUAL UNFOLDMENT IV

*T*HE ONLY *path for you is the way of confidence in God, in God's perfect wisdom. If you place your confidence in God, you are prepared to accept life as it is, knowing that it cannot be other than good; it is given to you in love, and all the circumstances of your life must be combining to bring good, to bring growth, to bring light and progress.*

To trust God means that you are absolutely at peace. You see life as a process of growth, and what appears so ugly and distressing you see as a condition which will ultimately bring beauty and perfection in the life of all.

If you have confidence in God you will remain untouched by anything the world can do. You will no longer be confused and troubled, once you have found confidence in God.

PRACTISING PEACE

The Right Pace

NOW patience is needed in this gradual journey towards unfoldment. You cannot jump over obstacles, as many people try to do. The ancient mystery teaching says that no candidate for initiation must try to rush forward. It is the lower self that wants to rush forward and get to the destination quickly. As soon as people awaken and consciously tread the spiritual path, they desire to know more and more. The mind becomes greedy for knowledge. This must be curbed. There must be self-discipline and tranquillity. Tranquillity is of the utmost importance, because the soul is only receptive to the ministry of angels in its tranquil moments. Many, many times the guardian angel draws close to the soul entrusted to its care, but when the soul is so concerned with the world and with itself it cannot receive the guidance.

So, if you would comprehend spiritual truth and divine law, you must follow your inner light; you must not only obey the voice of God within you but trust it, and even if you sometimes feel restive under the experiences which come to you, you must keep faith. You need faith in and obedience to the voice of God within; you need faith in that divine guiding light which is working through you. When you have achieved these virtues, you no longer question with your earthly mind the wisdom of God's laws. You surrender to the love of God, and you accept, accept, accept.

Against this, the earthly mind will pop up again and say, 'But surely I should accept nothing against

Thought

the reason that God, if there be a God, has given me'. How true! But the real reasoning power in you can always be satisfied by spiritual light. When light dawns in your heart, when through your own experience you have been drawn close to the heart of God or the Master, you both see and know. You do not then need books to tell you, nor yet anyone speaking as we are speaking to you. Your very experience in meditation, or in a state of contemplation or prayer, gives you something that can never be described; but in this experience, which is communion with your Creator, with God, you know truth.

If you are going on a journey to a distant country, usually you will make some effort to find out as much as you can about it. You will probably obtain maps and guidebooks, which will help you by giving directions on how to get there and by describing the country to which you are going. Beyond that they can do nothing. They cannot provide you with the means of transport, they cannot travel for you. You have actually to travel, to experience for yourself, and thus learn so much more than you can ever learn from maps and guidebooks. We are trying to make plain that when you are quickened in spirit, knowing that you have come from afar and are embarked on a long journey, then you are ready to experience all the beauty laid out before and all around you. You can experience the joy of your physical state and can breathe in the divine life forces in fuller consciousness. You must experience every detail of life with all your senses, physical, mental and spiritual.

Stand Against Ignorance

CAN MEN and women ever understand that God intends them to be happy? That God does not punish them but rather that they inflict their own punishment on themselves? You bring forward arguments galore in order to deny this simple eternal truth; you cannot bear to be told that you are your own enemy, and that you bring your troubles to yourselves. Yet when, through contact outgiving of love, you have learnt to go into the heart of God, into the Christ heart, trouble has no longer any power over you. Only when you become bound down to earth are you immersed in trouble.

We are not advising you to try to rise into realms of glory to the neglect of your duties on earth. But if you reach a state of spiritual receptivity you will see everything in the correct perspective, and understand true values. You will understand that all the things that trouble you really matter very little. All you have to do is to deal day by day with little difficulties as they arise, remembering that there is a wisdom ever watching over you, bringing about harmony and making crooked places straight for you.

Many people do not admit the reality of divine intelligence: they think that humanity has to battle for itself. Certainly you have to do *your* part, to work and to strive upwards, but also you have to recognize, humbly, that underneath are the everlasting arms, and that your Creator is merciful and loving. Those who have this realization find happiness and peace in spite of all difficulties. Their faith carries them forward.

This brings us to the question, 'How can we best

Thought

27

help humanity to overcome its fear of war, and destruction?'. A great mountain of fear seems to be building up, and because of this, people think out more and more terrible weapons by which to protect themselves. These thoughts of fear build up an invisible foe far worse than the one you can see.

Yet there is really nothing for the human spirit to fear. While they concentrate only upon physical things, upon resulting pain and suffering, people feel tortured because they can do nothing; their hearts are wrung and they lose poise and faith. But if you are really reaching out towards God, if you are living with love in your heart, nothing can touch you.

You must realize that imagination plays a very important part in life; it is a gift which must be striven after and cultivated, but at the same time imagination of the negative kind can inflict unnecessary suffering. A constructive, positive imagination can be a friend and helper, a negative imagination a foe. We would not make you disregardful of suffering, but we would like to say that the human body is so wonderfully constructed and the power of love is so great that there is a mercy which dims even the worst pain; and that love can and does work miracles. God is merciful as well as just, and as you probe the meaning of suffering you will recognize a merciful and loving power that succours and saves....

When the spirit rises above the body, the soul does not suffer. Do not allow this to make you indifferent to pain, for anyone who suffers needs all your love and your care; but we point out to you that the human spirit can rise above suffering, as Jesus demonstrated.

So we come back to humanity's fear of annihilation,

whether through nuclear war or ecological disaster, and again we beg you to remember that there is a loving, protective power. There is a plan for humankind outside which it cannot stray; the child of God has to learn to trust that power. God the Mother knows Her child and can apply an antidote to suffering, even as a human mother has an antidote to her child's suffering, and wisdom is guiding its tottering steps.

In the dawn of life, souls were taught by the angelic messengers and by the light within them to worship the mother element. The great Mother was the adored one; but times changed and the worship of the Mother was forgotten.

Now times are changing yet again; and more and more, in days to come, humanity will come to recognize and to worship the Mother aspect of God, divine Mother, and to realize the nature of Her blessing and Her influence. More and more leadership of and service to the world by women will be realized, and through this the true balance of life will be restored. This perfect partnership, this true brotherhood/sisterhood of the spirit, is coming. But it must start with the individual. As the individual man and woman expand in spiritual consciousness, so the whole community will become harmonized.

With the coming of spiritual enlightenment there must be a strong stand against the attack, not of a physical enemy, but of ignorance; for ignorance brings fear. And liberation from fear will come through your centering upon the light of the great Sun, the Christ spirit, Son of the Father–Mother God. As men and women learn how to open their consciousness to that spiritual light and life, all fear will depart, and they will grow in love and in confidence in each other.

Noble Truths

THREE points we now have in mind. The first is right thought; the second is right action; and the third is right living. The last two rest upon the foundation of the first point, right thought. The power of thought, the extent of the influence of right thought, is beyond human comprehension. Of course, right thought is always based upon God; it is God-thought, good-thought. You have heard the saying that thoughts are things. What you think today, you become tomorrow. You thus create or re-create your body, your life, your soul, and build your spiritual achievement, through right thought. Many people will not accept this and make no effort to discipline their thought, for it requires self-discipline. When we say this, many questions will come crowding into your mind, particularly into the lower mind, tending to deny the truth of our statement. But remember the importance of a steady 'keeping on keeping on'. It is the one who sees his or her goal and works towards it that attains both perfection and happiness.

While good thought is our ideal, it can only be put into practice according to your state of development, according to the laws that govern your life. We must recognize and submit in humility to the cosmic laws of reincarnation and of karma (or cause and effect).

It is not easy for the average person to recognize profound and fundamental truth, particularly when

*The Best
of White
Eagle*

he or she is functioning through the limitation of the earthly mind. A person must probe deeper than the ordinary mind in order to glimpse the justice as well as the love demonstrated in the law of reincarnation. Through reincarnation, you have the opportunity of fulfilling the law of cause and effect, although you do not necessarily have to reincarnate. We mean by this that you do not necessarily work out your karma in your next life or in your several future lives. You may be working out your karma of yesterday today. You may have sown the seeds of your present state of ill-health, or of your unhappiness and maybe disturbed and unruly emotions in this present life, several years ago. Now you are reaping what you have previously sown. You must not blame God for these things. You must look within; examine yourself humbly and honestly and admit mistakes when you see them. If you cannot recognize your own weaknesses, pray that you may soon be shown them.

We do not say anything in harshness. We come back in order to help you, not to judge you, nor to condemn anyone. We come with love, to offer you wisdom gained by experience.

Now the first commandment is *Thou shalt love the Lord thy God with all thy heart, and with all thy soul, and with all thy mind.* You shall love good and you shall be one-pointed in your love for God. This brings us back again to our first point, God-thought. Your life should be lived in God-thought, with the thought of good, looking for good, believing in good, trusting in good, constantly holding good thought about life generally, and about your neighbour. You must live always seeing the better, the good side, never the negative. You will be surprised at what will result. When you feel little aches and pains, instead of encouraging and nurturing them, put in their place a perfect thought, a God-thought. We know that this is a gospel of perfection, but we also know that until you put this into daily practice, you will continue in muddle and confusion.

We are giving you principles. The first is: always think well, always think good, eschew evil and all negative things. Seek only for God, for good in your thoughts.

Now for the next point: put right thought first. Control thought, thinking what you will to think, not letting thought run riot. Control it, train it, direct thought by power of the spirit, the holiness which is deep within your soul. When the thoughts are controlled and directed rightly towards God, there must come a natural prompting towards right action. If the thought be right, the act must be right. Right action is God action.

A Breathing Practice

BREATHE in the holy breath, the perfect breath of life. Breathe out the blessing of love. Practise this rhythm of holy breathing, breathing in the life of the Creator. Let it flow through your whole being, harmonizing, adjusting, purifying, ennobling your whole life. Your Father–Mother in heaven knows your thoughts, your prayers, your strength and your weakness, and has one thought only for you; it is that you should realize His–Her love for you. God does not want you to suffer or to be unhappy, but wants you to be at peace because you know your creator and your creator's power.

Do not think of God as a universal power without intelligence or love or personality. God still takes form and comes among you, and you must look for your creator in form everywhere in your life. *Seek and ye shall find.* God comes to you especially in the forms of the illumined ones, the elder brethren, and in the form of the Golden One. God has created you in His—Her own image, and possessed of infinite possibilities. *Be ye therefore perfect, even as your Father which is in heaven is perfect.* Say to yourself every morning: 'I am perfect as my Father–Mother created me perfect. I am divine love. I am divine peace'. When you go to sleep at night let your last thought be of praise and thankfulness to God. Think of crossing the river to the world of light. Let the divine will within you be your director both in sleep and waking. Do not look about you on the earth plane for inharmony and for those who hurt you and who are rough and unkind. Look above them. Keep your thoughts always fixed upon the good, the true and the beautiful God-life. Breathe in the breath of God. Breathe out the blessing of love and healing upon the earth. You, the child of God, are whole, you are holy, and as you truly and earnestly think, so you become.

Vision

NEVER mind what happens on the outer plane. Keep your vision on the light of God, for it is by the light of the God within you that you are able to look forward and catch a glimpse of the glorious light rising behind the mountains. When you have seen that, nothing will deter you from pressing forward on the

Thought

path which leads to that sunlight. You will long with all your being to grow nearer to the Eternal Sun, to feel its warmth and comfort and glory. Nothing will matter to you but that you become enfolded in it, so that you, being part of the one eternal life, may hold all life in your heart. Then slowly and imperceptibly the flame within the heart will grow brighter and more powerful; slowly and imperceptibly will dawn an awareness, a consciousness of the higher worlds in which you live. Slowly and imperceptibly you will begin to feel an at-one-ment with God, and the most perfect happiness, most satisfying joy which sickness will not touch, which death will not destroy but only enhance. There will come ever-increasing awareness of spirit which will accompany you through the portals of this world into the next, and through the next into the heavenly state of bliss. You will be helped by your guardian angel, the angel of karma, to follow the path of service and renunciation, of sacrifice and love. The peace of heaven will bless and fill you, restoring you to harmony and tranquillity. Let the captain, you, command the boat at all times. Cast out fear—there is nothing to fear when you love God.

FOLLOW where the Star leads you. Rise above the entanglements of the lower mind and the material world, and steadfastly and positively concentrate your heart upon the shining Star which is above you. Look right into it…. Feel yourself drawn into it. Rest in the consciousness of that shining Star.

THE BOOK OF STAR LIGHT

3. Meditation

THE POWER of thought is the creative power of all life. The mind must be stilled, and the spirit must become aware.

THE BOAT of your soul rocks in a great storm. When the soul calls rightly the Master hears. In you rises the divine power which causes you to be still, to be tranquil. Be at peace. Your Master takes over control of your boat—which is your soul—and you become calm.

TREASURES OF THE MASTER WITHIN

IN YOUR daily life you can, by an effort of the will of God within you, instantly attain, under any conditions, tranquillity of mind. Whatever the conditions, you can still the storm and know tranquillity.... Be tranquil and serene. A Master is never perturbed.

THE QUIET MIND

Constant Contact with Spirit

Y OU WILL find nothing more beautiful than you can find in your own inner temple. Grow strong in this simple truth. The innermost secret of life is to abide in the place of stillness; in tranquillity of spirit. Do not separate yourself at any time from this power; let it be a living force in you. Remember it is possible to withdraw into the innermost even if you are walking the streets of a great city. You do not need to enter into a quiet place, although it is better to shut away the world when you wish to get into contact with the Infinite. It is possible for the body to perform its duties almost automatically on the outer plane whilst prayer is taking place within.

It is wiser so to live that at any moment, in any place, you can pray, opening your heart to the great silence, to the Infinite, to eternity, and ask for help. Ask that the principle of love may be expressed through you in your dealings with your fellow men and women. We emphasize the necessity for your loyalty to the inward voice of the spirit, your highest self. If man and woman would only be true and loyal to the light, to the love within the heart, each, as an individual, but better still, in a community, could heal and cleanse the whole of humankind.

From the Heart

W HEN you can consciously contact the true Source of your being, the true Source of life, power flows into you and shines through you.

Harmony enters into your life. This gives you a new outlook, so that those things which once upset and hurt you no longer affect the peace of your heart. Usually men and women are filled with conflict, but if they can withdraw from all those difficult conditions which bind them and seek the Source of harmony within the self, the lifestream from God pours through them, and their material conditions are gradually and surely brought into harmony. All wrongs are righted when the consciousness of God is alive in the heart.

Through meditation and quiet contemplation the outer layers of the mind and emotion are gradually laid aside and the mind rests in the innermost place of stillness where the jewel of truth lies, the jewel within the lotus of the heart. This is *the light which lighteth every man*, the Christ the Son of God within. Search for it, my brethren, but not with a great deal of noise and talk; just quietly keep on keeping on, searching in the stillness of your own innermost being.

The mind must be stilled, and the spirit must become aware, must become conscious of its being. Then the human soul becomes illumined with divine spirit and consciousness expands into worlds of beauty and truth that bring peace and joy to the human soul.

Safety

HUMANITY sometimes thinks that all the good that happens in this world has originated from itself, failing to realize that collectively and individually, human beings are only instruments for spiritual and unseen forces that permeate their earthly life. But the human has one quality that sets him or her apart: the possession of freewill and the right to exercise it. The human has power of choice; the human can respond to all that is good and lovely, or may turn his back on these things and by following the path of self, reap nothing but disillusion and confusion.

Perhaps you will query this? You may be feeling particularly worried today, careworn, anxious, fearful. If so, just pause and think; try to look back over your past years. Review the troubles and trials through which you have safely passed, remembering too your periods of happiness. Then realize how you have been safely brought through your troubles. Realize that God has never left you without help, never left you alone. Always, something has come along which has improved your conditions. Even if you cannot admit that your material conditions have improved, have you not learned lessons that have brought you some ease of mind, some mastery over self? Are you not wiser? And even if you have suffered loss, has there not been some development, some unfoldment of your spiritual nature? Through your difficulties, trials and sorrows, light has entered into you; your consciousness of a divine love and a guiding hand has grown as the result of past events.

It is therefore a mistake ever to fear the future when it can bring an ever-increasing consciousness of God, an ever-unfolding understanding of God and God's life. It is equally mistaken to fear death. There is no death! We are always saying this. Some, and perhaps most of you, think that you believe it. You day, 'Oh yes, we know that there is no death!' But you do not know it sufficiently. You lack the deep realization, and the spontaneous reaction that you should have towards eternal life.

Service

A S YOU think, so you become; and so you create the conditions that surround you. You must learn to use your good thought. Within you all is this divine creative principle which has the power to create vibration among, and to control, the actual atoms of matter. We tell you this to help you, for all have the divine urge to know and to become aware of a life which is free, which is holy, happy, healthy and joyous, a life in which you can render service to the world and in which you can see quite clearly the Land of Light. If you would have a better world, create it for yourselves now at this very instant in your mind: hold the thought there continually. Refuse to allow any other thought to banish it from your consciousness, and then raise your whole vibrations and your aspirations. It does no good to dwell on darkness.

So many of our friends make the mistake of descending to the level of conflict in their minds. They think of the worst; they see the worst; they allow themselves to be drawn into conversation about the worst that might happen. Remember that every negative thought goes out into the universe and adds to the sum of negative thought in the whole of life. Remember also, however, that the same applies to good thought. A brother–sister of the light dwells in the spirit, sees good, and knows that all works together for good. If you train yourselves to think positively of good, to see good and believe in good, you are serving the whole of creation. You are raising the life consciousness of all creation. Your little contribution to the whole is of enormous importance.

Never allow yourselves to dwell in darkness or fear or inharmony. If you will transfer your thoughts from physical matter to spiritual life, you will solve your problems. This is a truth, even if it is one you cannot appreciate at present. Nevertheless, practise what we say. Do not think about physical conditions or problems of the earth. Think about God and you will be with God; you will be in God's kingdom. Do not allow your thoughts to limit your life, or the life-force which continually flows into you. You limit this power by negative thoughts, but its flow increases in you and in your life when you attune your thoughts to the Star.

Thought is a living thing, and it can be increased in effectiveness by the power of prayer, and faith, and hard work. You do not sit down and say, 'Dear God, provide for me'. You say, 'I have a pair of hands, here am I. Lead me to my work wherever it may lie'. You set in motion a thought, and if it is a good thought it attracts the spiritual atoms. It goes on working, not only physically, but in people's hearts and souls. *Nothing in your life is so important as your God-thought.* Your best work, both for your own happiness and health and for your service to humankind, will be done if you will close all the doors of your 'lodge'— by which we mean the holy space you create within and around you. Do not allow the negative thoughts and destructive vibrations of the outer world to penetrate it. You may think this selfish and self-centred, but it is not so. It is the reverse, for it means that you are becoming strong within; you are learning to become a master—master of your own body, master of your own lodge. It also means that you can give far greater healing and light and strength to the suffering people in the world to help them overcome their difficulties. Instead of your being sucked down into chaos and darkness, you are becoming strong to help.

Your mortal mind will have many arguments against our words. We know; oh, we understand, but we remind you that you have a divine mind as well as a mind of earth! Bring this mind into action. See the perfect life, the life that *we* know in the world of spirit; a life wherein all have learnt to work together for the good of the whole. This is the creative goodness that you can project into your world. Look up to the light and become great channels for the light, and refuse to listen to the mind when it tempts you to give way to despondency. Keep the light burning steadily in your heart.

You can still the storm, you can become serene and still. You can bring forth the higher life in your own being. In your daily life you can attain tranquillity of mind instantly. It is difficult, we know, but to be able to do it you must keep on practising. Every day, before you start your daily work, practise centring yourself, even if only for five minutes. Stop your outer activity. Send your thoughts to those in spirit who are watching and helping you. Let this spiritual life become a living thing, so that it is always with you.

Practise the presence of God, even if only for five minutes in the morning and a few minutes before sleep. Relax mind and body and quietly and slowly breathe deeply. As you breathe in, try to imagine that you are breathing in light and life; that you are not only inhaling air, you are filling every particle of your being with light. As you do this, you will forget your body, and you will be freed from earthly problems. You will, if only for a fleeting moment, be released from the bondage of care and limitation. As this love fills your heart and your mind, every atom, every cell of your body will be filled with perfect life.

Emotional Control

L ET US consider the inner world of which we speak. To you it will appear a mental world, because when you withdraw from the outer, the physical life, you seem to go inward. Then it appears you are living in your mind. However, this inner world is not only a world of thought, but also a world of feeling. You are getting beneath thought, and thus you come to a world of finer feeling, or an emotional world. Although they may not realize it, all people live in such a world of emotion, yet this emotional life is also affected by the mental world around them, or by the thoughts of others. It therefore becomes part of your training or development of spiritual insight, of clairvoyance and illumination, for you to learn to protect your fine emotional body from the harsh thoughts of the outer world. For you are unconsciously influenced by the thoughts of others. You will feel the effect in your solar plexus without knowing what is happening. Maybe you put it down to some physical cause. We are not suggesting, of course, that every upset of this nature is due to such emotional impact, but it sometimes happens. Then you need to protect yourself from thoughts that can penetrate your aura and affect this sensitive place, the centre at the solar plexus.

The way to protect yourself from receiving these arrows of thought is to steady your emotions, to control the emotional body. This is not easy, but it is essential if you wish to approach the higher planes, if you want to draw close to those higher brethren who are waiting to help you. You must prepare yourself to come within their aura. To do this, you must control your own emotional body, and this is where so many aspirants fail. They try hard, but their emotions are too unruly and so they keep themselves away from that calm, beautiful place where the master minds, the master souls dwell. We want you to think well about this because it is one of the very first lessons to be learned—the recognition of the reality of this emotional plane, of your own emotional, your feeling body.

You see from this that to protect yourself against the thoughts of people that disturb your emotional body you must seek the love of God, the love of Christ. You must pray for, and strive to be, this gentle love. In the degree that you can call forth that mild, peaceful, tranquil love in your heart towards life—not only to people but towards life itself, so that you are radiating love—you are encircling your aura with a white shield which is impenetrable by the world. Unwanted thoughts cannot penetrate your aura if you have sent forth love from the temple, the centre in your heart. If your emotions are controlled, calm and lovely, you cannot be affected, nor your mind be disturbed, by thoughts from the world. A master has complete control of circumstances through having gained mastery of his or her own being.

Those who want to develop the sixth sense of true intuition in order to work for the Master must rule their emotions. Sometimes the soul needs pain and suffering, both to develop the deeper emotions as well as to learn to control them. But the middle way is the way for the disciple—a ready response in the feelings to the sufferings of others, and to the spiritual influences which come to help the soul. Unruly emotions are a hindrance to the one who is seeking the development of the intuition.

The emotions are always symbolized by water. When water is turbulent, you get a false reflection. If the water is calm, clear and pure, you get perfect reflections from above. So when the soul has trained itself to be still and peaceful, it is receptive to the true impressions, true feelings from spiritual worlds. Lack of mental control is the greatest hindrance in the Master's service. Peace is the achievement of controlled and wisely-directed emotion. The razor's edge upon which the disciple has to walk is to develop feeling, but also to control it.

The Perfect Flower

Imagine, if you will, a lovely gentle rose on the central altar of a temple, opening its petals to the sun. A rose is the symbol of a human heart fragrant with love. You may not often see hearts like this, but we do. We see many human hearts open to us and can inhale the perfume of sweet human love. Give out that same perfume yourselves. Withhold judgment and criticism. Remember the trials and the difficulties in another person's life which may make them irritable and sharp. Turn away wrath by gentleness and love, remembering that as you feel hurt and irritation, so may your companion feel too; and until you can feel with the feeling of your companion, you cannot be a master soul. The human way is to judge in haste the action of others, but the divine way is to remain quiet and loving.

So, with this symbol of the rose in your midst, be very still, be at peace…. At this celestial level of consciousness, you should develop the power to receive truth, the power of feeling and imagination. If you feel the beauty of the heaven worlds, you are receiving divine truth through your intuition. This is how you can discriminate between the divine will and self-will. The disciple leaves all earthly things—mind, body, possessions, desires—to follow God. Having reached this understanding, you can safely rely upon your intuition. It all comes to these few simple words: *'Be still* (in love) *and know that I am God'.*

Your whole life is lived within a concentration of cosmic forces, and like a magnet you attract to yourself conditions and powers like those you have awakened in yourself. All substance of whatever plane of life can be humanly moulded: by your thought, by your will, you can mould this substance into form. When you have really gained mastery over the physical body, the nervous system and the thinking—so that in all ways you can create the condition that the divine will within you wishes to create—then you are able, when you sit in meditation, to build round you 'the temple of the Golden Flower', exquisitely formed of spiritual or celestial substance. In meditation you are fully open like a beautiful flower, like the thousand-petalled lotus of the head chakra, or the many-petalled lotus of the heart chakra. You as a spirit are actually in that flower, and that flower builds up all around you in the form of a most beautiful temple, a spiritual temple. You are then in the temple of your own soul and spiritual world.

Through the blending of the intellect and the emotions the spirit is touched, the intuition reached. The feelings plus the thought-power open up the intelligence of the individual, as distinct from bare intellect, which cannot alone digest or deal with the food of the spirit. Controlled and wisely used, the emotions will so well interpenetrate the mind that the intuition and the divine intelligence can operate.

The Mind in the Heart

IN THE spirit world is a beautiful garden, and everything which grows therein is an expression of the spirit of God; the flowers and trees, their colouring and perfume, the song of the birds and the play of the fountains, the layout of the garden itself, are all manifestations of the highest and purest Godlike thought. Angels help to create this garden. In the centre of the garden is a lake of crystal water reflecting the sky and the flowers and trees, and the reflection makes the garden even lovelier. As the garden is reflected in the still waters of the lake, so is truth reflected in the individual heart. But to reflect truth, the heart must be tranquil, serene and still.

The mind of itself cannot understand or know truth, for the mind is so often a turbulent sea at the mercy of the emotions, the likes, the dislikes and the passions of life. The mind can be as an arrogant dictator seeing no wrong in itself. Truth can only reflect in such a mind in broken fragments; this is why earthly people fail to understand the plan of God in the world.

But the mind of the heart, like the still pool at the centre of the garden, reflects pure truth from the mind of God. You can look into the pool and see the law of cause and effect at work, can see the reason for all that happens and the perfection of God's plan for the ultimate good and progress of all humankind.

Standing by this lake and watching the reflection of goodness and beauty, you see your own reflection too; you see yourself as you are, in comparison with the beauty and glory of God and the manifestation of God's truth. And then you gain the jewel of truth....

THE LIGHT of your lamp shines forth more brightly when you are serene, when you have learnt to control the passions of fear, anger and hatred. You must learn to reach these spheres of serenity continually, for there lies the power of good. It is through the children of earth that God works miracles.

WHITE EAGLE'S LITTLE BOOK OF HEALING COMFORT

4. Kinship

WE ARE
endeavouring to
awaken in each
one of you an
awareness of the vast
brotherhood of life.

*L*ET US *in spirit worship God in silence, under
the heavenly canopy of stars; let us commune
with the spirits of the air and the fire and the water
and the beautiful earth.*

*The peace of the eternal love and harmony fills
our being. May we feel the air of the higher spheres
blowing upon us, and may our eyes be opened to
the company of the invisible, and the presence of
the perfect One.*

PRAYER, MINDFULNESS & INNER CHANGE

*Y*OU WANT *to listen to the spirit world, to listen
to the words of love spoken by your beloved in
the beyond, by your guide, your teacher, and later
by your master? Learn then to listen first to people
on the earth, to give your whole attention to the one
who is speaking to you; listen also to the sounds of
the birds and animals, the song of the wind in the
trees, of the falling raindrops and the rushing river.
This is how the Native Americans were trained
from childhood; and because they were so trained,
they were able to hear not only physical sounds, but
sounds behind those of earth, the sounds of the
unseen world. They could distinguish the voices
of their spirit guides and teachers; they could also
hear the nature spirits. It is difficult for you in these
noisy cities to hear anything of these, yet you must
train yourself to listen.*

PRACTISING PEACE

*The Best
of White
Eagle*

The Ancient Wisdom

BEHIND all religions through the ages is one truth. This is the ancient wisdom, brought to humanity in the beginning by God-beings, messengers of the Great White Brotherhood. If you study this ancient wisdom, you will recognize how its influence pervades all religions. It comes to light again and yet again in many a re-presentation. Whatever the forms or the symbols used to set forth truth, when you go back to the foundation you will find there the seeds of ancient belief, the ancient wisdom. As it was in the beginning, is now and ever shall be. Ancient wisdom sets forth a plan of life which embraces heaven and earth; as it is above, in the heavens, so it manifests below, on the earth. It is the wisdom of the heart; it enshrines knowledge of the divine fires and creative powers with which all are endowed, and of the divine laws which govern all life.

Fundamental to the ancient wisdom is belief in a supreme being, God, known by many different names in different religions, but as the Great Spirit to the American Indians. The Indian who worshipped the Great Spirit worshipped the whole creation of Almighty Being. The noble Indian gazed at the sky with thankfulness and recognized a Power there. The Indian recognized it in the stars and the planets, in the Sun and the moon, for he or she knew that the planets and stars had a great influence upon the earth and upon his own life. The Indian studied the ways of nature, studied the winds and the rain clouds and the four seasons. Indians recognized that behind all these natural forces there was a directing power with

Kinship

which they could work in harmony, and bring peace and happiness in their own lives by obeying the Great Law as taught by those that came before.

Ancient wisdom teaches that behind the physical Sun is the spiritual Sun or the white light, and the ancients were taught how to use and direct this white light for the blessing of their life on earth. They were taught how to work with the angels to control the elements. They learned how to make contact mentally and spiritually with the forces of nature, and how to live and work in harmony with them.

They were taught, for instance, how in the act of breathing in the fresh air they could also establish contact with the angels of light. An angel is a messenger from God, therefore these angels or nature forces were able to direct rays of light—power, wisdom and love—to those with knowledge, and through certain practices (notably in meditation and in their way of life) these Indians were able to form very true and beautiful links with those natural forces, and even with the great devas themselves.

As you unfold spiritually, you will be able to see, even as the ancients did, the spirits of the air: the sylphs and tiny fairies. You will see the angels of the water element, and those lesser spirits who work under their command—the water sprites, the undines. You will see the spirits associated with the earth element—the fairies and the gnomes. The ancient peoples were helped by these angelic powers and nature beings to enrich the soil by the power of the spirit. They had the secret of how to work within natural law to maintain the fertility of the soil, and in ceremonies, perambulations and invocations they called down the invisible forces to bless their lives. In these invisible forces they knew there were vast armies of nature spirits whose co-operation they invoked.

Looking back, my brethren, down our path of life, we have a memory: the picture of an ancient American life, of a time when the brethren were all united in love, when they understood and worshipped the Great Spirit. Because they had touched the centre of life, they comprehended the power in that life and in the light, and they knew that without a supply of the heavenly food Mother Earth would become exhausted. So these ancient Indian brethren used to gather on the plain to invoke the blessing of the Almighty Spirit.

That same white light can still be called down, gathered in to the earth to give nutriment, not only to help the grain to burst and send forth its shoot; but also to make it grow to perfection. Those of you who have gardens, and who are lovers of nature, will remember what we say that the finest fertilizer you can give to your crops is the white light, the love of God.

The Inner Life of Nature

L OVE your flowers, my brethren; talk to them, and talk to your brother trees. Our Native American brothers and sisters used to talk to the spirit of the trees, and the flowers, to the running water; they talked to the Great Spirit in the mountains—all life manifested the Great Spirit to them. Be friendly with your little field daisies, with the flowers of the hedgerows, even with the very blades of grass. Try to feel the kinship you share with every living creature. Even

Kinship

the minerals are alive with the light of God. Each wayside stone is vibrating with a light and life it shares with every plant that grow. If you had clear vision, you would see that all the flowers and trees in your garden are pulsating, vibrating with colour and life.

The earth is imbued with the divine fire of life. This divine fire, which is also called love, is the life in everything. If your vision were clear, you would see the divine fire even within inanimate things: metal, stones, wood, are all pulsating with tiny sparks of light, of fire. All nature is pulsating with this divine life.

The colours in the flowers are brought to them by the fairies, the nature spirits, who are working through the central stems of the plants, pouring in their own essence according to the need of the flowers. In other words, the flower is taking upon itself the colour of the fairy creature working with it; the essence, the quality of the consciousness of the fairy, is being expressed through the particular flower.

If you could look at a tree with your spiritual eyes open you would see more than its trunk, limbs and foliage. You would see the fire within the earth and in the roots of the tree; you would see the fire rising up through the trunk of the tree to radiate light through all its branches and leaves, particularly in the spring of the year. The divine fire is shining not only in the sky, in the rays of the sun, but in the earth itself and in all nature.

Not only is this inner or etheric world vibrating with colour, sound and perfume, but interpenetrating all are the rays of the planets. Certain parts of your body vibrate in harmony with certain planets, for every planet has its correspondence in your being. Try to understand and receive these vibrations more fully into your being. When you have learnt to vibrate in tune with all life, you will have attained mastership.

Refreshment

WHEN YOU look up at the sky at night, and gaze at the countless stars, you think you are looking on a vast universe—but you know nothing of the unseen life within that universe. Physical eye cannot see nor physical brain comprehend the immensity of that invisible universe. Yet if you are learning to enter the stillness within your simple heart, you can begin to understand; to become aware of that vast invisible universe.

If you will walk in your garden in this state of inner stillness you will become aware of other creatures, apart from the human, apart from the animal and apart from the vegetable lines of creation. Be still; withdraw into your temple of silence. If only for a flash, you may see numberless little nature spirits, flower fairies, gnomes. Even the very stones are inhabited by etheric folk. Yet in the ordinary way all you see is the outer form of pretty flowers. If you stop to think, you will wonder how the flowers are brought to blossom, what brings their perfume, what is it that makes one flower yellow, another pink, and the leaves green. What is the power that lies behind this?

Behind all nature are beings great and small working under the direction and control of an angel on one of the seven Rays. These beings work automatically under their group angel, although they have a degree of choice and latitude, and they are continually carrying life-force to beautify the form and colour of your flowers.

Exactly the same process takes place in every department of life. Your physical body is in the charge of what your psychologist describes as the instinctive mind, or what we have referred to as the automatic mind. Sleeping and waking, the functions of the body go on and are controlled by the instinctive mind, which in its turn is under the control of a great angel being. Angels attend you from the moment of conception until the time when the silver cord is cut and you leave the mortal coil for a span, to return for refreshment to the heaven worlds.

When you are refreshed, and it is seen that the time is right for you to return to the vineyard, you return to incarnation to do some more work, to labour again on the spiritual path. How you labour is your own choice, but you must live always with this thought, 'I have come to the earth to serve life, to serve the grand scheme of the evolution of humankind'. You live and move and have your being in a spiritual universe, and have your part to play in it.

Perspective

YOU wonder why we emphasize the beauty of life, and apparently ignore that which is inharmonious and unbeautiful. From your earthly point of view you may feel a little rebellious, thinking, 'Oh, why emphasize the so little beauty and ignore the overwhelming sorrow and ignorance and darkness?'

It is because we can see so much more than you can of the transcendent beauty of the spiritual life, and of mortal life also. Even while we are speaking to you now we hear the song of the birds in the trees outside this building, as music to our souls. We feel the companionship of these flowers on the altar; we see the forms of the nature spirits who guard them, and are responsible for their beauty and fragrance. These little nature spirits are our companions, our brothers.

What a glorious world! Leaving the city, we can go into fields of wild flowers, see freshly shooting corn and trees laden with the promise of fruit. We see in the skies countless millions of nature spirits, all working together for the good of life, and to bring gifts of food and sustenance to humanity. We see all around you in this chapel the forms of radiant teachers and angelic beings, waiting to serve, to fill your souls with love and peace. We see that through the music you have heard, the angels of music are drawn close to serve you, touching your souls as hands play upon a harp, so that you also may absorb the harmony of the spheres of music.

Do you wonder, then, that we continually emphasize the gifts of God, poured forth so liberally upon you, God's children? Do you not see that in the degree that you respond to love and beauty, so you are increasing beauty on earth; and by the same token decreasing that which lies on the other side of the scale—the darkness and ignorance and bitterness and selfishness of humanity?

We know the sordidness and ugliness in human life, but it is our work and yours to dispel that

Kinship

sordidness. We move forward on a path leading us ever upward and onward towards the kingdom of heaven; and by every thought and act in our daily life we can create joy, happiness and love, and thus help forward God's great plan of evolution.

Harmony

WE HAVE another very important message for you: we ask you to concentrate on beauty. We have a very good reason for saying this. The earth is grey, and at times there is a dark mist on your earth. We won't say any more, just say there is a dark mist—and there is so much ugliness on earth. There is ugliness of speech, of sound, of buildings— ugliness in so many departments of life. What we all have to do is to create beauty.

Beauty is a spiritual food—beauty of form; beauty in nature, in Mother Earth; beauty in colour, in movement, in music, in thought, in expression. All these aspects of beauty are so important. By your concentration upon beauty—in your surroundings, in yourself, in your thoughts—try to convey beauty into the lives of others around you. See perfection, ignore all the ignorant chatter.

When you work from the spirit you are creating beauty and helping humankind to absorb and to express beauty, in all its forms. You who have been trained to meditate see beauty because you are working from your innermost spirit. Imagine the world of spirit, think of the beauty of colour and form and sound, think of the music, the harmony of the spheres; when you are attuning yourselves to the higher life, to the spirit world, you should always hold a picture which is beautiful.

The most ideal subjects for meditation are to be found in nature. You may visualize the mountains, the still lake or pool in the temple gardens in the spirit world, or the beautiful garden of flowers. All these natural scenes have an effect upon your soul. They bring you into rapport with the Great Spirit. In the infinite and eternal garden you will see angelic forces, forms with human faces, in colours unmatched on earth, still and peaceful—continually giving, giving, giving help, pouring love and wisdom upon creation. We suggest that in your meditations you always concentrate, as far as you are able, upon the Great Spirit, and then upon the beauty of nature.

This form of meditation is very simple, but the more you repeat it, the more it will help you in your work. If you begin by concentrating on beauty in all its forms, we assure you that you are not neglecting suffering, or the inequalities of life. Give from your heart the perfect love and see your beautiful world cleansed of all pollution. See the beautiful earth used by humanity according to the Law of God—humankind giving back to the land what they receive from it.

Do you not feel as we speak the harmony of this circle of life? No one can form any idea of the grandeur and the beauty of the infinite scheme. There is no such thing in all creation as splendid isolation; no separation between any form of life, but all is blended in one harmonious whole. What appears to be error, evil, destructiveness, has behind it the great power, wisdom and love outworking through the whole plan, bringing good out of apparent evil, guiding and linking up every form of life.

This is a grand thought: all is working together for good and nothing can harm the one who loves goodness and truth. You are increasing the light over the whole of this planet. Always be ready to go forward with the power of the spirit which enters your soul; go forward in faith to enter into eternal peace and joy and happiness, and when this planet becomes a planet of light, which it will, it will become a shining star in the heavens.

You are on a path of eternal progress. You will enter into the golden world of God.

In a Circle around the Fire

WE SHOULD like you to come with us on a journey.... Close your eyes, close your senses to the outer world, and imagine that we are all sitting around a camp fire under a starlit sky with the brotherhood of nature. The scene we depict is in fact quite familiar to many of you, and it will not be very difficult for you to go back in memory to the times when we all assembled in a large circle, sitting upon Mother Earth, watching the campfire burning in our midst, smelling the perfume of the earth and the pines and the flowers and the woods; looking up to the canopy of heaven, gazing upon the twinkling stars. These were more to the Indian brothers than little lights in the sky, for they represented the powers of God which can destroy and recreate. We learnt to accept all that God sent to us as being good, for we understood that the Great White Spirit, all love and wisdom, was in supreme command, we knew that the great planetary beings and angels, right down to our nature spirits, all obeyed the command of the Great White Spirit.

Picture, then, all the brethren gathered in the hush of the evening, listening to the orchestra of nature: the wind in the pines, the murmur of the insects and faint twitter of birds and little cries of furry beasts, beaver and rat and all the tiny creatures of the water and woods—all one great happy brotherhood, living under the protection and by the love of the invisible power, the Great White Spirit. Even as we gazed up into the heavens, to the stars, they spoke to our innermost heart of love, of brotherhood, of peace....

In this present cycle and in your generation, you are so clothed with civilization that you are shut away from this contact, through nature, with the Great White Spirit; and because you are cut off from the direct contact with nature, you suffer from nerve strain, which sometimes develops into disease.... And still the soul longs for this unknown comfort and strength from the Source of life. You endeavour to contact this glorious Spirit through your mind, but in the old days we tapped it directly through our senses. Humankind has again to learn the use of the five senses, for through the five senses (which are allied to vortices of power in the etheric body) can be drawn wonderful spiritual power and life-force.

Through imagination then, through using the sense of smell, the sense of touch, the sense of hearing, of taste and sight on the etheric plane, let us contact nature here, around our camp fire.

We are endeavouring to awaken in each one of

Kinship

you an awareness of the vast brotherhood of life. Seated in a circle around our fire, we feel in our innermost being a living peace, and true brotherhood and unity. Let us radiate this peace, a creative power, into the ether, that it may find a resting place in the deep subconscious mind of humanity.

Do you see? Oh, we beg you to see them: the small furry creatures, the beaver, the rats with bright eyes, dormice, frogs and the little creatures of the earth. See them all around us, all joining in with our brotherhood; even owls and sleepy birds, all one. Even the crackle of the fire is causing the salamanders to leap about, and nearby at the river we can hear the splash of the water sprites; we hear the wind in the trees, and the spirits of the air are winging their way to join our brotherhood. Peace on earth ... goodwill to all life.

Prayer

*O*UR BRETHREN, *we feel the life of the Great Spirit not through our mind, but through our senses, both physical and etheric.*
All around us are the pine trees—symbolizing peace, aspiration and strength... and the music of the wind breathes its message to heart and to mind: the Great White Spirit is brooding over all creatures ... all is well.

PRAYER, MINDFULNESS AND INNER CHANGE

5. Karma

THE WISE man or woman resigns all in perfect confidence and faith to the exact outworking of the law of God, of love.

*W*E ASSURE *you, with all the love that is in our hearts for you, that the only way is the way of love. Let little things go; put them in their right perspective. Little things can become like mountains, but they can be very easily disposed of if you disregard them and train yourself to regard only the big things, the important things. Give way on little things that do not matter, but on matters of principle stand firm as a rock.*

PRACTISING PEACE

Forgiveness

WE ARE all human and we all fail at times and need forgiveness. In the spirit world all have to be very forgiving. So will you also try to forgive those who err, who make mistakes largely because they do not understand? Forgive them also even if they do understand according to your knowledge. Forgiveness in your heart brings sunshine, peace of soul and tranquillity into your life. Forgive, therefore, not only the big debts, but trivial human frailties. When hasty emotions threaten to overwhelm you, just forgive. Then all shall be forgiven you, and God will bless you.

The second quality is thankfulness. Never cease to feel thankful to God. This is the secret of a perfect life, for in the act of thanking you become in tune with God.

Thank God for all the blessings of your life, and for every opportunity offered to you during this incarnation which enables you to grow nearer to Christhood. Do not let your days slip by aimlessly, but be ever on the lookout for the meaning behind every episode which comes along. Life is not something just to be muddled through, but given so that you may welcome and rejoice in every experience. These experiences are meant, not as a harsh chastisement or punishment, but as opportunities for you to learn to understand the wisdom of God's laws and the power of the spiritual light which emanates from God. Take with both hands what the world would call bitterness, for within that bitterness you will find the nectar, the sweetness.

It is the way in which you accept your experiences that matters; the way you allow them to awaken the love of the Christ spirit in your heart.

Karma

KARMA, my children, is really unlearned lessons. These lessons have to be faced in a calm spirit. Rejoice in your karma. Thank God for the opportunities which are presented to you to learn lessons and dispose of your karma, for these are steps by which you mount into the Great White Lodge above. Every piece of karma gone through means a lesson learned, but the most important thing for you to remember is *do not just try to get past your karma*: be sure you have learned the lesson which the episode was intended to teach. If you have not learnt the lesson and have just skirted around your karma, you have only put it on the shelf and it will come back again and again until the lesson has been learned.

Is this hard? But it is true, and we are trying to show you and to help you, because we love you. We are your companions. We have passed your way. We have ways to travel beyond and beyond and beyond the earth, but when we look upon karma, the obstacle-lessons which are placed before us, we accept them with thanksgiving. This is why we say, on many occasions: accept, accept, accept the conditions in your life and be thankful for them, for they are steps leading to illumination and perfect happiness.

The secret of the divine magic comes to you when you have overcome, when you have learnt to master the lower self and to manifest divine love, gentleness, kindness: when you have learnt not to retaliate or be resentful. The initiate resigns all injustice, however great or small, to divine law. He knows that the oil-press of the law crushes the olives, and the oil of wisdom remains. The hardships, the inequalities, the difficulties, the injustices of life are all ground in the press of God; and the pure oil of wisdom, the pure wine of life, remains.

The Laws of Life

WE WOULD remind you that human life is governed by spiritual law, by the law of cause and effect and also by the law of opportunity. In the East the first is called 'karma', the second 'dharma'.* You do not fully understand what these two laws mean in daily life. Now you have been given the gift of freewill, and many people feel that because they have freewill they are their own masters, and can do as they like. This is true. Nevertheless, the soul must be prepared to face the result of its actions. That is, if it chooses the way of selfishness and unkindness, it must be prepared to suffer the effects which will follow upon that desire.

However, the law of cause and effect goes hand in hand with the law of opportunity. Each time a cause is sown, like a seed, in the individual, or in the national or international life, there is bound to be a following effect, which can be either happy or unhappy. But, in any case, it will bring fresh opportunity, for the law of karma causes the law of dharma or opportunity to operate. In sorrow and in joy, remember that the outworking of your karma is bringing you an opportunity to acquire wisdom and thus step

*'Dharma' is often translated as 'the teaching'. White Eagle extends this to 'opportunity' in the sense of 'enlightened following of the path'.

forward on the path.... The cycle of life is moving upwards in a spiral. In spite of patches of darkness, which you call evil, humankind is progressing. A heavenly light is penetrating the minds of men and women, and their hearts are opening, one by one, reaching out towards love, goodwill, righteousness.

We in spirit can look upon the earth from an angle which you cannot. We can see into the hearts of people, and what we see is beautiful. We see goodness, we see the light of Christ growing. We also see that which is crying out for love, and this is where you can help. Remember, the divine Spirit has endowed you with the qualities of God's Son, the Christ. You have the power within to create your own heaven and to create your own hell; to create heaven or to create hell for your brother–sister on earth.

And so we say ... look to the spirit; let the spirit guide you in all your undertakings. Be true to your innermost light, and you will create heaven and know complete happiness on earth. Do not dismiss what we say with the excuse that it is no use only one person making the effort. The way to bring a golden age on earth is for every individual to be true to the light of the spirit of Christ within them. Put this into practice in your lives, and you will be amazed at the results.

Looking Forward Positively

In your own lives always look forward, anticipate good. By anticipating good, by anticipating blessings and happiness, you are actually drawing these to you; you are creating, through your imagination. Imagination is part of the psychic gift implanted in the human soul. Therefore, we say to you from spirit, use *your* heavenly imagination; imagine yourself in a state of perfect health, imagine yourself in a state of harmony. If your conditions are inharmonious, see them becoming smooth, better. Disciplined imagination is the key to creation.

Perhaps you are unaware that whenever you think negatively, you are actually creating negative conditions for yourselves. To create positive good, you must always think positively. If you do this habitually, you will clear the mists which gather round you, mists in your own soul, mists in your mind. The light of Christ in you, expressing itself through your positive thinking, can shine like a sun and dispel the mists.

We cannot impress upon you too strongly to think always in terms of progress, of happiness and of achievement; and you will become healthy and happy. This is our special message for you as you stand at the beginning of a new year. For as you creatively imagine your conditions so you are setting into operation the machinery which will bring about the very picture you hold in your mind. As you think light, as you think good, you will become a creator, with God, of a beautiful world, a beautiful humanity.

Initiation

THE SOUL receives continual opportunity to attain divine illumination. During its every incarnation, lessons are presented—call them tests if you like—which are actually opportunities for progress and initiation. Tests come to you in almost every detail of life. By these you can gauge the reactions

WHITE
EAGLE ON
LIVING IN
HARMONY
WITH THE
SPIRIT

of your emotions to human events, the reaction of your minds to life in general, and the reaction of your hearts in the love you feel towards other beings. Finally, through the tests you will recognize how you are bringing the divine attributes right through your physical nature, and your ability to direct and control your life by calling upon the supreme love, power, wisdom and intelligence of the Most High—your Creator.

Your life is charged with opportunities to grow in wisdom, love and divine power. Beloved, put your hand into the hand of God ... and He–She will lead you step by step. Make the effort to walk God's way and you will pass your tests and initiations (a word which means expansion of consciousness) until you become as one of the twenty-four elders around the throne.* Then as never before you will know the significance of the word 'humility'. Once you know humility you will strip yourself of your crown of light—which means that you will know that you are as nothing, for you move and have all your being in God. In God's life alone you can live and know supreme happiness beyond all earthly understanding.

This is the answer to the many who are so deeply troubled by life's contradictions. They ask, 'Why? Why? Why? What have I done, that this trouble should come to me?'. All we can reply is that you have either refrained from or needlessly neglected some opportunity to serve or to express kindness to your earthly companions. This is why the suffering came. You will go on to ask, 'What is the good of it all?', perhaps protesting that because you cannot remem-

*For the reference, see Revelation 4 : 10

ber what happened so long ago, the suffering fails in its object. To which we answer that if your physical brain cannot remember, your deeper consciousness knows well that it has earned the experience.

Be thankful, therefore, and accept all your opportunities disguised as so-called karma. Suppose a person goes through a particularly dark patch of trouble or sickness, or suffers a great loss, undergoes some kind of limitation or hardship, or meets misunderstanding or injustice. All these experiences, when seen in their right perspective—with understanding that they are lessons through which your master is trying to make you see and understand life more perfectly—all these will be recognized as tests. Furthermore, you will always find, however trifling a test may seem, that when it is passed, there has come a change. 'I shall never be the same again', you say. That is true, never the same, but always better, let us hope; for in a minor way an expansion of consciousness or understanding of human nature and human experience has been the result.

Let Go Futile Worries

CAST OUT fear, my children. There is nothing for you to fear. Fear is a weakness, a chink in your armour of light; if you are fearful you are opening a way for the enemies, the adversaries of God. You weaken yourself when you give way to fears either for yourself or for others. Have no fear; place your whole confidence in God, your Father–Mother.

Your difficulty on earth is that you want things to hurry up, you want things to happen all at once; but spiritual power works slowly. If you put a seed or a bulb in the ground it won't be hurried, it will take its time to grow and eventually bloom. This is how spiritual power works.

If you live tranquilly and patiently, always with the consciousness of God's love upholding you, you will find that all your life will be heaven. Whatever has crept into and seemingly spoilt your life will all gradually be resolved. But this won't happen if you harbour irritation, fear and chaos in your own heart. Let go these futile worries and fears. All things work together for good for the one who loves God. Your Father and Mother in heaven know your need. Why be anxious? Seek the inner silence, the stillness of the pure spirit. In this shall your strength lie.

*Y*OU *all have problems of one kind or another and many of you have fears for the future. Never cross your bridge before you come to it. If and when you come to it, you will be carried across with great power and love.*

THE SOURCE OF ALL OUR STRENGTH

6. Teacher and Pupil

YOUR LIFE
is charged with
opportunities to
grow in wisdom, love
and divine power.

*Y*OU WILL *always be hearing from us:* Keep on keeping on. *So many cannot do this. They go to sleep by the wayside. They get discouraged. They turn back. But the soul who perseveres and keeps on keeping on reaches the goal of spiritual liberation.*

TREASURES OF THE MASTER WITHIN

The Journey of Life

THE PATH of life on which you have set your feet is high and steep but it is not unconquerable. Many have climbed this path before you, some are half-way up, some are right at the top, but those who are at the top are not unmindful of you and your efforts. They come unseen, unheard, to give you strength, to give you light, to enfold you in their love.

The work of every soul in incarnation is to learn how to manifest the love and the beauty of God. And these companions of your spirit whom you have known in former lives are with you to help you. They guide you and help you to learn your lessons; they are with you in sorrow and perplexity to strengthen you and in joy to help you to be happy.

You are tempted to resort to the weakness and error of the lower mind and of the material world. But instead of being overcome by these temptations of the lower self, each time you respond to the light of the higher self, or respond to the prompting of your guide, who fills your being with love and humility, so you will grow stronger. Then you take a step forward and upward towards your goal.

Yet still the journey seems long and you become discouraged, and begin to think you will never reach the golden heaven. We know, we know; but we come to bring you good cheer, for joy must be your companion on this path leading to the heart of God. We understand the weariness of the flesh, we understand the soul-weariness, but we know too that there comes without fail a sustaining, refreshing grace to uphold the weary traveller on the journey.

We bring you a message, not only of joy and hope, but of assurance that God's love is omnipotent, omniscient, omnipresent; and it is for you to receive it as a welcome and honoured guest, into your heart.

Tending the Flame

IN THE process of evolution humanity as a whole has for a long time concentrated upon self as it journeys upward—and necessarily so. Each individual has had to become self-conscious; but self-consciousness will give place in time to the consciousness of God within. God-consciousness has three main modes of expression—power, wisdom and love.

Many today long to find a way of service, so that they can help to relieve suffering, and help those coming on behind them towards harmony and happiness. The path is not easy to find at first, and being found, is difficult to walk steadfastly. There is so much to confuse the aspirant, and when he or she has found the path, so much to draw the aspirant off it. You may ask, 'How is the path to be found?'. First by entering the chamber within, and praying for wisdom. When presently the light comes, it will not be due to any mental stimulation, but will be born from the heart....

In the mystery schools of the past the pupil was led by his or her guide to the door of the temple of wisdom. The pupil knocked on the door (do you remember the words of the beloved Master, *Seek, and ye shall find; knock and it shall be opened unto you*?) and sought admittance to the temple, where he or she was tested very severely before he or she could proceed. Today, you also knock upon the door—

not physically but in your spirit. Something in your heart stirs. You long for wisdom, for understanding: you long to serve, and to know how you may serve. The Master hears your cry, and you are accepted as a pupil—and then the testing comes. You are almost daily confronted by the tests which your higher self has sought, but which the outer self, in ignorance, rejects and grumbles at.

The real you, the soul which is stirring, awakening, searching, has asked that you may be tested, that all manner of difficulties should fall across your path. In the trials that beset you, always remember that your higher consciousness has asked for the light, is seeking initiation. The first awakening comes when the soul realizes that it has the choice between good and evil. Next, when the soul knocks again at the door of the temple, the crying need is for light. It cries out for light so that it can see the path before it. It comes in utter darkness, bound by the material world, and cries out for light. So the pupil enters, and after being put through certain tests is given what his or her soul longs for: the light is awakened within, so that the pupil dimly sees his or her place in the great plan. At the same time the soul is permitted to catch a fleeting vision of the light towards which it journeys. Faint though the light within is at first, it sheds a ray, and other wayfarers who meet the pupil on the path, who also have been through that testing, recognize the soul's light, as he or she too sees theirs. The elder brethren, when they look down upon earth as though looking into a dark night, see little lights twinkling like stars. These are they in whom the light has been kindled—and you, no doubt, are numbered among them.

Immediately a soul sets forth on its quest, passes its test and shows forth the little gleam of light, the teacher comes. The light is a signal to the masters, to the teachers, and to those angel beings who watch the destinies of humanity; they know the need of the child of God, and they come to assist the spirit within to become stronger, brighter, to bring the whole being towards perfection.

Beloved children, sometimes the little light waxes strong; sometimes it flickers till it seems almost as though it might go out altogether, but this it never does. It is buffeted sometimes, and the heart within the brother or sister grows weak; but as we watch, we fan the flame, and try to give strength and courage to the pilgrim on his or her way. And remember that although we speak from the spirit realms, we too are walking the path, and we too have walked over the roughest stones, even as you have, and as you are still doing. The path is no easier for one soul than another. All must tread the same road, the road of daily sacrifice, daily putting self a little more on one side, daily resisting the temptations of the lower self. Do not think that your task is any harder than that of those who have gone before, for all have trod the selfsame road.

To See with Eyes Freed from Confusion

WHATEVER problem you now face, face it in the light of Christ, and do not allow thoughts of fear or misunderstanding to cramp and blind you. Look into the face of the master, the gentle wise elder brother, and strive daily to live in thought, in company with him. And you will find that conditions will be made clear for you, the path before you will be straightened out. Strive to live above the materiality of the world.

There are two strata of life: the earth plane, where there is darkness and confusion; and above, the land of light, in which you may dwell if you turn your back upon the error and darkness of the material level of life, and concentrate heart and mind upon the land of light. Do not think that this is a land of illusion, for it is real, and by living with your head in the sunshine (not in the clouds!) you will be living in a land of reality. We do not want our earthly brethren to have their heads in clouds, we want them to have their heads in the sunlight. It does not render you impractical to live in this way. On the contrary, it makes you more efficient, with all your senses bright and gives you clarity of thought. Keep your head in the sunlight, and your feet upon beloved Mother Earth, walking the green carpet of earth, so soft and springy, which is comforting, which is like home.

May your life be like this! And it can be. It does not depend upon outer conditions, poverty or wealth, friendship or companionship. It depends only upon you and your relationship with … *the light of God.* You will have all things if you will become *truly* at one with love, which is Christ. *I, if I be lifted up from the earth, will draw all men unto me.* Raise the Christ in yourself, and all those with whom you associate will be lifted up with you.

Vision on the Star

EACH one of you has your own particular fear, and what you on earth would call a little trouble. No one on earth is completely without some problem; it may seem only a small problem to others, but a very big one to you. Now we want you to consider this question of fear and loneliness and the problems that affect you in your daily life, sometimes very deeply. We want you to understand that we of the Brotherhood of the Great White Light who dwell in the world of spirit and the celestial world are not without knowledge of your particular difficulty. We love you and want to help you. Many of you were companions of ours in former lives and we feel the relationship between ourselves and you. You think only of your present incarnation, and many of you may think that you live through threescore years and ten and then you are finished. Oh no, you are far from finished—you have only just begun! Life is not just for threescore years and ten, but for eternity, and is continually unfolding.

A wonderful provision has been made for you and every human being by a wise and loving Father–Mother God, and this provision is that there are periods in your life when you leave your hard work on earth and withdraw from the physical into a heavenly state, and there in that world of beauty and harmony you are refreshed and strengthened. You on earth cannot conceive of the beauty that awaits you in what your orthodox friends call heaven. You know how you all feel after you have had a lovely holiday—you return to work feeling full of energy and strength and ready to continue your very interesting work. This is the point: your *interesting* work.

Some of you feel that your work is far from interesting, that it is wearying and boring, but you alone can make your life's work interesting, and will do so if you are seeking for the blessing of all life. Whatever your chosen task or whatever work God has placed before you we say—accept it with thankfulness. Do your best and God will do the rest. It is for you to make the best of whatever conditions you are in. Make the best of life, be thankful for life itself, and keep your vision on a goal, which is all good.

WHITE
EAGLE ON
FESTIVALS
AND
CELEBRA-
TIONS

Now you all come to a point at some time or another in your life when you have an ordeal before you and you are afraid. Fear is humanity's greatest enemy. You fear your ordeal, you fear perhaps an operation or a big change in your life, you fear changing conditions because you know that you are entering the unknown. Most people fear death, because they do not know the meaning of death. We in spirit have passed through death many times—and so have you, but your memory is blocked because you are in the valley. If you had risen to the heights you would have a clearer vision and you would know that there is no death, only a change of condition, only a different state of life. There is nothing to fear in death, for you do not die.

If you look back over your life you will know that what you most feared never happened. You found yourself facing an ordeal you could not avoid, but when it came to the point there was a most heavenly power that carried you unscathed through the experience you dreaded.

We want you to think about this because it will help you to make your contact in full consciousness with the Great Spirit, with that all-enfolding love which teaches you that all is well for the one who loves God. A child has to trust its parent, and the parent must be worthy of that trust. Each person's own experience teaches him or her to trust the divine parents, because again and again it is proved that God is all wise, God *is* love, and that what comes to each in life comes because of the divine law which is love. When you break the law of love you are unhappy, you are distraught, you are fearful. You fight to escape the dilemma, not realizing that there is this law of love and, when the person obeys it, when he or she applies it to daily life, all problems dissolve. There are no problems, only God is there. Most people fear change, and when change comes, they wonder what is going to happen to them. Instead they could feel, 'God is wise, I place my hand in the hand of God, knowing that all change is for my good'. When all people know this then the world will reflect the kingdom of heaven....

Always remember to apply divine law to your problems. If you do this, you can never go wrong.

And so to old and young we say, 'Keep on keeping on, with squared shoulders and head high'. Keep right on to that world of light where there will be a great welcome for you in a beautiful home, in which you may rest for a while to gain refreshment before going forth once again to serve, and to love and be loved.

*A*ND HOW, *you ask, are we to walk the spiritual path? We answer: say little; love much; give all; judge no one; aspire to all that is pure and good—and keep on keeping on.*

THE QUIET MIND

7. Healing

YOU ARE light, and you have to shine out in the darkness.

R ISE *above the babble of the market square, and abide in the quiet places of the spirit. There you will hear the voices and know the companionship of the shining ones. If you can do this you will become a channel for the healing of people's souls and bodies.*

LIVING WITH LOVE

B E *sure that if you think aright, think creatively and positively, you are an instrument of God, for you set into operation the law of the divine love, and the results will be wholly good. This is the form which true healing takes.*

HEALING THE WORLD

The Best of White Eagle

Angels of Healing

VERY little is known at present on the earth plane about the angels of healing, but as the age advances, many more people will not only feel their presence, they will see them. According to the need, according to the vibration created, so there come to a healing service the angels of different colours clothed in the light of the sun. You know that the sunlight is full of the colours of the spectrum; now think of the angels of healing in these beautiful colours. There is nothing dark or ugly. They are all light and purity. These angel beings draw very close to the healer, who contributes the substance which they need to establish contact with those who have sought the healing power. These healing rays can be used to heal not only the physical body of an individual, but also the mind and the dark material conditions which oppress humanity.

The radiation of the pure white magic flowed continually from the heart of Jesus. Anyone can still receive in their heart this same radiation from the heart of the Christ; and if their heart remains pure and joyous it can in turn radiate light and healing to all the world.

Spiritual healing is a great work in its spontaneous selflessness. The healer does not think of his or her own aggrandizement. The healer who did so could not heal. He or she thinks only of the good of others; thinks only of the alleviation of pain and suffering; of the transmutation of the dense conditions of life into a more heavenly state of being.

So we would say that if you long for spiritual

development, for unfoldment of spiritual vision, give yourself in service to heal the sick. The Christ through Jesus of Nazareth said, *Feed my lambs*. Feed the sick souls of your companions, through spiritual service, spiritual healing. Thus you will be serving selflessly not only present but future generations; you will be helping God to create a better state of life for all people on earth.

My children, follow the path of service, of true goodness, spontaneous joy in life, and become, in time—like your beloved Master Jesus the Christ—perfect sons and daughters of the living God.

Intuition

THE GREAT white light of Christ is the healer of all ills of body and of soul. It heals the physical body, and is the great solvent of all shadows. It is ever the builder, ever the constructor, and you are called by the hosts invisible into service with the light, into action.

'How'—we hear your unspoken question—'How can we serve, how should we act?' You must endeavour to become aware of the invisible forces which are playing upon the earth life. You must train your body and your higher vehicles to become consciously aware of this stream of light which finds entrance into your being through the psychic centres; you must learn to be aware of this circulating light stream which vivifies and can glorify body and soul, and pass from you, directed by your highest self, to heal the sick throughout the world—the sick in body and mind. The vibrations and the power of the angels and the great spiritual beings work through human channels to build heaven into the human consciousness. This is the temple training of the past, according to the ancient wisdom; becoming aware of the land of light, becoming aware of the light within the soul; of the effect of colour upon the soul, upon the mind, upon the body... the effect of perfume ... the effect of sound.

The time has now come for you all to develop your sixth sense, which we call intuition. Humanity has for long concentrated upon the stimulation and development of intellect. This sixth sense, or ray of light, is destined to open for you the secrets of nature, of creation, and all spiritual life and purpose. We ourselves work especially on this ray of intuition, the love–wisdom ray. And so when you and we and the company of spiritual brethren meet together in the inner sanctuary, we meet in love, desiring one of the most precious gifts of life—wisdom, through love.

The unfoldment of the psychic or spiritual centres can be quickened by love in the heart, but development of love without knowledge is not enough. If you are only sending out love, you can get into a complacent, dreamy state; but with the opening of the higher centres you can work with knowledge. Knowledge should be coupled with love, love with wisdom; it is necessary to develop the wisdom aspect. We know that all things can be done with love; but if you do not get knowledge, love can be compared to the flower which has not opened. Strive for knowledge; strive for full consciousness and understanding of what you are doing in the higher planes.

In your meditation, you are being taught how to bring the higher chakras to life: that is, how to open your consciousness to the pure, the spiritual level of life. This is the right way to unfold the inner faculties. The sixth sense, the intuition, functions from the heart centre. In meditation, in true contemplation of the Deity and all that is holy, you are opening up that centre. The safe way and the correct way for spiritual unfoldment is to work from the heart of love. The soul-consciousness is situated in the brain. The divine spirit, we suggest, dwells in the heart. You are opening the throat centre, too, for pure speech and knowledge—knowledge which comes from the fifth sphere, the sphere of Mercury. With the development of the throat centre comes inspiration for speech.

The One who is the light, the Christ within, lives in the heart centre. The physical organ—the heart— bears a sacred relationship to the spiritual centre in the etheric body situated over the heart. When death takes place, the divine spark, the seed-atom of the spirit, is withdrawn from the heart. When this is understood, it can be readily accepted that the life of the spirit functions through the heart centre. It is called love. Your heart then, is the centre of intuition.

As we speak to you, one great truth which occurs to you is the need to contact, not only mentally but spiritually, the eternal truths of life—a contact made with the mind of the heart. Many schools find the intellectual way is their path; it is so because the intellect has need to grow and expand. But there are those in incarnation who do not need to pass along the intellectual path in order to gain or absorb the eternal truths. Many find the way of the heart easier, and certainly we work on the love–wisdom ray. So we would reveal, not in words alone, but in essence, the glorious light of the spirit.

There are many ways of learning the inner mysteries, not necessarily through the written or spoken words. If the soul can attune itself to higher planes of love and wisdom, the mind in the heart will absorb; and although the outer mind does not always immediately interpret the truth thus absorbed, nevertheless later the mind will begin to interpret and in time know great truths, for the heart does not register incorrectly. That which the heart absorbs is truth. In this present age this sense of intuition is developing; through the intuition, hitherto insoluble truths will be solved—truths insoluble to the materialist, however great the intellect. The mind of the heart will know, will understand, these greater mysteries.

One example of this is how the memory of previous incarnations can be recalled, as the soul strives to reach the higher consciousness, outside the limitations of the physical brain. With many people, it is just a nebulous feeling. Or it may be that the soul is aware of certain tastes and characteristics brought back from the past—love of embroidery from China, love of dancing from Greece or Spain, love of Egyptian art. Some little trait in the character may betray a link with some past civilization. These memories do not come through the earthly brain, so much as through the spiritual brain, centred in the heart. It is through the mind in the heart that contact with eternity is made. It is almost another name for intuition.

So the intuition has to be developed. Mistakes do not matter. In comparison with the greater and wiser ones, we all make mistakes. Certainly it is right to strive to develop the intuition, but make sure that the inner voice comes from the heart of wisdom, and not from the self that wants something, the desire self. Intuition comes like a flash, it is an inward knowing. The thing is to have courage to act on it; to be prepared for whatever it brings. The intuition can be developed in meditation, not through activity of the mind, but through quiet contemplation within the sanctuary of the heart.

A Higher Level of Being
The higher self is composed of very fine ether and is pulsating with light, which as you develop will begin to shine through the chakras in the etheric body, the 'windows of your soul'.

When this divine fire is brought into full operation so that all the chakras are active as God intended, then the whole body will be in a state of ascension. We mean by this that the whole body, although still of a physical nature, will be functioning on a much higher plane of consciousness than it is at present. At present it may be in a dark state, but when the divine fire is kindled and active, then the body will be quickened in vibration and will be light and beautiful. It will approach the standard achieved by the God-beings, the Sun-beings, who walked this earth in the beginning of its creation.

You are here to use physical matter, and not allow it to dominate you. You are here; you are light; and *you* have to shine out through the darkness. You have to use your physical life and raise it, to transmute the heavy atoms of the physical body.

Within you lies the power to change the very atoms of your body, for the physical atoms are the spiritual atoms. These tiny sparks of light are the power behind all visible form. These atoms can be changed by the command of God. The whole of life is under the direction and command of the Great White Light.

Healing is the intake into the body of the eternal Sun, the light. If you can call upon this light, breathe it in, if you can live consciously in this light, it will actually control the cells of the physical body. The body is so heavy, material life so strong—but do not forget the power of God to recreate the living cells of your body.

When we said earlier that there would be a new planet born from the heart of the Sun or Son, we meant that from every life will be born a new world. This is beyond your comprehension at present, perhaps, but remember that you are all sons and daughters of God, and will become gods, from whom will be born a new world.

As they grow in spirit, the people will no longer fear death. The people will not even know death, because they will be quickened to life in the spirit. Death with all its morbid trappings will be a thing of the past. When men and women have finished their period of service they will withdraw from the physical body to a place for refreshment in the heavens, still retaining full consciousness of life in all its fullness, both on earth and in the spiritual sphere. Death will be overcome by the spiritual life. Death will be swallowed up in victory, in immortality; because when men and women learn to live by the true spirit, recognizing in each other the same spirit as that within themselves, they will know that there is no separation by death.

Love

A SPIRITUAL healer who is attuned to God is able to bring to the patient the stimulus of the love ray, the power of love. Healing is really by love. When we say love, we mean dynamic love—the Will of the Father being expressed through the Son, through the healer. *The Father that dwelleth in me, he doeth the works.*

In the past, the healer would call upon the subconscious or the psyche of the patient, call to it and talk to it. That is what psychological healing is doing today. But also, just as you can talk to the subconscious, you can also call to the Christ within to quicken.... You may like to think of the body as composed of so many atoms or cells, and that in each cell is a spark of God that can be called upon to perfect the body.

True love is the key, the secret. All wise men and women, all the saints, know this. You will find throughout the ages that the key lies in the heart. The key is simple love, true love: but not an emotional gushing forth! That is not love; love is the will of the Father–Mother. Love is *doing* the will of the Mother–Father which sent you: that is the key.

Above the Mists

CAN YOU define love? When we think of love, we at once feel an outflowing, a giving, to you, to all life. To love means to give. When you love you seem to go outwards, flow out in order to help, to serve. But as you cannot breathe out without breathing in, so you cannot give love without receiving. Love is an out-breathing and an in-breathing. It is a light that burns deep within; a warmth, a certainty, an inner knowing. Whenever you are not acting, speaking or thinking in love, you are unhappy because you are out of harmony. The earthly mind will not usually admit this. It goes to extremes to justify itself, but the inner you knows that you are out of harmony when you are not feeling this emotion of love. Love is God; and God is discovered within the heart. If love is absent you flounder about and cannot understand the meaning of God, and God remains a mystery.

The divine essence that is love is God, is the Creator. God is love, and all life and all form is created by love, on whatever level love operates. Let us say here that form is not only created on the physical plane, but on other levels of life. Is it possible that form can be created in the spirit world? Most certainly. Is a woman to be denied the joy of motherhood in the spirit world? Why should she be? As below, so above; as above, so below. If she longs to hold her babe in her arms, that joy awaits her in the spirit life.

Each one of you is accompanied by an illumined soul from the world of light—a guide, companion or teacher—and certainly by the one who is the affinity of your spirit, for where love is there is no separation. So, my children, if your particular loved companion is in spirit life, try to realize that the etheric bridge can be crossed, for truly angels and your loved ones can come to you once you have raised your consciousness to them.

Try to realize this truth within yourself; to realize that you can create the bridge by love, by your belief in God's love, by your belief in love itself. When doubts assail you, remember that they are only the promptings of your lower mind, or what you are sometimes pleased to call 'reason'. It is only the lower, material self that cuts you off from those you love who live in the land of light.

This message is specially for those who feel the need of comfort, who want reassurance of the continued companionship of a loved one, for we can see many troubled hearts; we can see loneliness and in some cases almost a despairing spirit. We would not materialize the spiritual life, or try to give you proof to satisfy your physical senses. But we pray that we may raise you to that level where you may become aware of the life of spirit.

There are people who declare it impossible for those in Heaven to reach those on earth, saying that those in a heavenly state are forever cut off from earthly life. But they are only cut off if you yourselves do the cutting. If you are unfolding your spiritual life, you will naturally rise heavenward and those in heaven will come halfway to meet you. It is the Creator's will that the sons and daughters of God should learn to penetrate the heavy mists surrounding them on earth, mists of selfishness and materialism which obscure the heavenly world.

The lower self holds you down to physical matter. But by right living and right thinking, by aspiration and even by the way of crucifixion, you can find your way to the heavenly state. Once there, you find truth.

You find truth through love. It may be through love of nature, love of beauty, love of music, love of another human being, love of God; but your love for God will be the same as your love for humanity, because you will find and love your God in humankind.

Before Sleep: a Healing Meditation

NOW CLOSE your eyes, close your senses to all earthly things, come with us in spirit and see that we have brought you into a Temple of Healing, indescribable in earth language. All we can tell you is that it is radiating all the colours of the spectrum, gentle, sweet colours. Shall we liken it to a pearl?

We are in the Temple of the pearl ray; its tall columns rise right up into the heaven.... But it isn't so much the perfection of the architecture that impresses us, as the perfect harmony and beauty that we feel....

Imagine this perfect healing temple, and you will see it; you will feel the glory of this life here in spirit. It is for you, it is part of you, my child.... How can you be anxious and worried about earthly things, when you have seen and know that true life, which is working all things together to produce good in humankind?

Try to live in this consciousness always, always. Withdraw from the noise and the babble of the outer world. Go into this temple, kneel in simple prayer before the communion table and receive from your Lord and Master the sacrament ... the bread and the wine.

Rise with renewed strength and go forward, in company with your loved ones in spirit. Even if your work is of a very material nature, in a very worldly world, even in this you are helped and guided. Never forget that each one of you is watched over. Your soul-need is known. So open your heart in simple trust, and all the crooked places will be made straight.

*B*EHIND *you is a power beyond your comprehension; God only waits for you to be willing to be a channel. God only waits for you to serve, knowing that of yourself you are nothing. May the channel open wide and the light flood through! By your mental direction it can go forth to heal the nations, to heal the whole world.*

THE QUIET MIND

8. Others

ONCE YOU have
reached an affinity of
spirit, you have touched
the whole sphere of
love, and you will find
and recognize in all
humanity that
same love.

*G*O ABOUT *the world being love, being caring, not only to those who are more congenial to you, but to all men and women. Do not fall into the error of regarding anyone at all as your enemy. No man or woman is your enemy, all are your teachers.*

THE SOURCE OF ALL OUR STRENGTH

*O*NE OF *the lessons all souls have to learn is the lesson of love. Personal love of a selfless nature is beautiful and it makes life lovely and brings great happiness. But the personal love must be broad and wide. Love, like power, must be poised; it must be steady; it must in a sense be impersonal. You may think that impersonal love is cold, but this is not so. Impersonal love is pure and without condemnation; it is all-embracing, all-enfolding, all tenderness. Above all, it is love without pain.... Learn to love without pain, then, and you will have learnt the main lesson love has to teach. Is it hard? Yes, to you on earth all these things seem hard, but that rich reward which follows the learning of the lesson on earth is worth the struggle.*

LIVING WITH LOVE

I am in God; God is in Me

THE LOVE, the light in the heart is pure spirit, the seed of God; and human life must be guided by the spirit. You make your affairs so complicated with the little mind of earth. But goodness is so simple. Learn, my dear ones, to be guided by the spirit, which is the love within you.

Be wise and allow nothing to disturb you. Care neither for praise nor blame, and do not grieve, either for the living or for the dead. Know that the divine law is just, perfect and true, and that that law must work out in every human life. So never grumble or be discontented with your lot. If you will train yourselves to accept your karma, realizing that you have much to gain from it, you will be able to live so much more happily.

The most powerful instrument for help is prayer, used with sincerity and humility. Pray for one single thing, which is God's love; pray for an increase of God's light, not only for yourself but in order that others may benefit and be blessed. Pray for God, pray for good, and resign all to God.

Uniqueness

WHEN you confuse sentiment with love, you create a difficulty, because sentiment has its place, and it is not easy to separate it from love. But like all virtues, when carried to excess, love loses all its power. It becomes a hindrance, and may allow someone to sidetrack: to cover up their own weaknesses and faults in the name of love, and to become blind to the real need of their brother or sister. Perhaps this is one of the most important things we have to say: that misplaced love, or sentiment, can blind you to your real service to your brother, to your sister; it will cause you to give unwisely—to indulge, not only yourself, indirectly, but others also.

We use the illustration of the devoted mother, who gives the child everything it demands. Thinking this to be love, the mother not only bestows the things her child needs, but, blinding herself to the child's need for self-development, gives it all things, material, mental and spiritual. What is the result? Instead of giving her child opportunities to grow and so be happy, the mother is robbing it of every chance of self-expression and development. The wise mother, by contrast, withholds lavish expenditure on every plane.

Does this mean that the mother should become cold and indifferent? No. It means that the mother has such love that she sees clearly the child's need for experience, that it must learn to make its own decisions. The mother and father, if they are together in mind and heart (and we do indeed hope they are) must together watch not only the bodily growth of their child but the mental; they must note carefully the games that are played, the books that are appreciated, and particularly how the child thinks about what is around him or her. We deplore the tendency at school to push in material facts until the poor brain is stuffed full and stultified. We would rather encourage the child to grow in spirit, to open like a flower in the spiritual powers. Again, we repeat, the purpose of life is growth, and at the present age, the growth of the spirit of the child is particularly necessary.

This is where you need discrimination. All children are not alike. The best and finest way for the parent to assist the 'coming in' of the self to the young body is for the parent to endeavour to attune himself or herself to the spiritual life. Much indeed is absorbed by the child from the aura of its parent. Sympathy, discrimination, and love: mother love must not be overdone, or it may degenerate into 'smother' love, so that the beautiful incoming self is driven back and the desires of the little body of flesh over-indulged. Then the body takes predominance over the spirit. Remember, it is the spirit you would assist.

Now, love is wisdom. If so-called love has no wisdom, it ceases to be love. True love is wise and just. True love wants spiritual growth, and true and wise love knows that experiences are necessary for the child's growth. Love also knows the soul has come back with certain karmic debts to be erased, therefore mother love will not strive to prevent their working out, nor shield the little one from all the winds and the rains of life. Rather it bestows courage, a clear outlook, and noble bearing, so that the child may meet all like a sturdy little plant, unswayed and unbroken. It helps the little plant to thrive in all weathers, until at last it turns the bloom of its spirit to the sunlight, to the light of the Master, the Lord Christ and God its Father and Mother.

You may wonder, when we talk about the need for wisdom, where the service you believe you have to give begins and ends. Sometimes, people seem to make such high demands. We would remind you that you are here to *learn* wisdom. Your heart is full, it is loving, but that is not enough by itself. You must strive for poise, inner strength and wisdom. It may help you if we tell you that it is kinder to the other person to withhold sometimes.

It is much harder for you to withhold than it is for you to give, so sometimes the lesson you have to learn is to withhold. But there is a way of withholding. The uninitiated will withhold with a selfish and greedy motive. As you develop on the spiritual path, you will withhold with a good motive—not because you want to deny the other person your service, but because you want to help them in the right way. You do not always help a soul by giving too much. On the contrary, you may spoil that soul. You have to be a teacher of the soul and the teacher must sometimes withhold in order to give the best possible help to the pupil.

Wisdom is the counterpart of love. Wisdom is love; love is wisdom. If you have not wisdom, you have not complete love. If you will try to picture the figure of Christ, the Perfect Son of God, and absorb from that picture the qualities of the Christ, you will find it will be a great help. When service is demanded of you, just pause for a moment and say to yourself, 'What would the Master do here?—is this really helping?'. And if the answer is that it is not helping, then ask for strength to say no. There are always two ways of doing things—the kind and the unkind way. Always choose the kind way of saying no. That is simple. The great Beloved One said, *Whosoever shall not receive the kingdom of God as a little child, he shall not enter therein*, and we say that the great soul is the simple soul. We have all proved this, have we not? The greater the soul, the simpler.

Personal and Divine Love

THE FOUNDATION of all spiritual growth is love. We all like to love and be loved; it is natural and makes life joyous and comfortable. Many of us, however, do not understand love unless we see it manifesting through a human personality, and this is quite right; for did not the great Master say, *He that loveth not his brother whom he hath seen, how can he love God whom he hath not seen?*

But sometimes the affection, or the emotion, called love is centred largely upon one person. Is this good? Only in so far as the personality is recognized as a window through which true love shines.

To find the root of love we must reach behind all personality and recognize a quality of life which is universal. When we touch the place of true love there is no separation, there is no question of separating any individual from his brother, her sister, because all the children of God become one when we truly love. This is difficult, for you will argue that in human life you must centre love upon individuals; that your best love must be reserved for husband, wife, children, friends, sweethearts, those who are nearest and dearest, and that your love for them is of a different quality from that which you feel for others.

You will feel more in harmony, perhaps, more at home, more comfortable with those nearest and dearest to you—that is, for ordinary purposes, for ordinary life, because your nearest and dearest minister to your body and comfort your mind, and separation brings grievous loss; but once you have reached beyond the earthly to the spiritual compan-

Others

ionship, to an affinity of spirit, you have touched the whole sphere of love, and you will find and recognize in all humanity that same love which is shown to you through the individual.

In every individual soul there dwells the divine life, that life which you all have in common, and it is that which enables you to feel the emotion of love. Therefore to know the meaning of love we must all seek to find that divine love in all our comrades, and not make the mistake of limiting love to any one individual. This seems a paradox. Through loving the individual you contact divine love, and not in any other way. Until you have mastered this lesson you cannot know what real love is. We see the light shining through individual souls; but in reality we love, not the individual itself, but the quality of love shining through. No teacher will ever claim personal love. Did not the Master Jesus continually remind his disciples of this truth? *The words that I speak unto you I speak not of myself: but the Father that dwelleth in me, he doeth the works.* The divine spark in you reveals the Christ to you.

Concentration

WHEN YOU meditate or pray, one of the best ways to prevent the intrusion of the daily mind is to treat the intruder with contempt. Ignore it. Concentrate more strength than ever upon the God within; and that concentration will become so absorbing and so powerful that the little outer mind will retreat, unable to overcome or penetrate the enormous battery of prayer to God. Do not worry about turning out the culprits. Just ignore them. Concentrate with all your strength and all your being upon God. Your concentration possesses you and fills you with power and light; everything else falls away and you become a living battery, a force of divine light.

WHITE
EAGLE
ON THE
INTUITION
AND INI-
TIATION

Similarly, every time a destructive thought comes into your mind in your everyday life, dismiss it at once. You may not recognize it, but this accumulation of destructive thought in the mental body of humankind eventually turns into ideas which create destructive weapons. Instead, you can so easily discipline yourselves to think and create forms of goodness, beauty and harmony.

It is just the same in dealing with the people around you. When you have little difficulties, it is far better to ignore and let them pass; concentrate on the power and strength of Christ within, and these foolish difficulties will disappear. Too much time is wasted on fussing and worrying about little details in your interpersonal relationships. Concentrate on God and the expression of the Christ within. Nothing else matters. You make mountains out of molehills. Remember, *Vengeance is Mine, I will repay, saith the Lord*. When you feel inclined to retaliate because you have suffered an injustice, don't—you can safely leave the working of the law of God to its originator. Justice will be enforced to the uttermost. It is the law.

Concentrate on God; nothing matters in life so much as this, because by concentrating on God and awakening the true faculties of your higher self you are doing all good. You are putting forth every effort in the finest and the truest way in life and on the earth plane. You

Others

need not bother about negative things. They automatically right themselves if you get to the centre of truth and God ... power, love, and knowledge.

The human soul has a freewill choice. Although it has to accept certain experiences which the angels of suffering are urging upon it, the soul also can respond to the angels of love. So the human soul, while it must experience suffering and sometimes pain and degradation, has always a good angel near to whisper, 'God is love. Look up, my brother, all is well! God enfolds you in His–Her love'. Thus in the midst of all human suffering is that little voice to which all can if they wish respond, which says, 'Hope, my sister; good will come out of this experience'. Look up, love God, love your Master and Christ. This is the freewill choice of everyone, this is the voice of Christ within that speaks. But remember also that no soul can escape experience that the angels of darkness will bring.

And so we want you to remember the words from your Bible: *Whatsoever things are true, whatsoever things are honest, whatsoever things are just, whatsoever things are pure, whatsoever things are lovely, whatsoever things are of good report ... think on these things.* Think good thoughts. Think God thoughts. You know it is a very wonderful gift that your Creator has given to you— the power to think, and the power to choose what you think. If you think God thoughts, you are not only sending them out into the world, but you are opening yourself to the inflow of more and more wisdom, heavenly wisdom. You are raising the vibration of all humanity; and as you do this you are developing your sensitivity—your power of clear vision and clear hearing, and your power of healing.

Blending Intellect and Feeling

What is an individual's protection, then, against the negative influences which surround the earth plane? A pure heart, pure loving aspirations, we would say. Your desires then are not of the lower nature, but of the true Self, the Christ within. The true self seeks to serve, and takes no thought for itself. It indeed has no time to think of its own progress, its own initiations, of that splendid moment when it will at last enter the Great White Lodge. It thinks not of these, but of how it can best serve and love those whom God sends within its orbit. Service, through love, is the focus of the true self.

How necessary it is to distinguish between love, which is wisdom, and emotionalism, which may disintegrate love! How necessary to recognize a love seeking not its own, opening wide its heart, thinking not harshly of that denomination or that sect, this sinner or that, not condemning, but accepting that in all planes the great scheme of God develops! Such love accepts that even in so-called 'evil' there is a purpose, for that which is called 'evil' in people's hearts is ever used by the Omnipotent to teach, through experience and through suffering, through the lesson of the cross to the moment of dawn, that people may see the sun rising upon the new age.

When carried away by joy or overwrought by pain, or at any time when you are emotionally overstressed, you are like a frail boat tossed about in a storm. Yet within everyone awaits the sleeping Master, the indwelling Christ. When at last you can call upon Him in your distress, crying 'Master, help me!' you are appealing not to any outside teacher but to the Christ

Others

within. You cry, 'O Thou who art light and power and love, come to my aid!' Then tranquillity steals over you. You are at last aware of an indwelling strength and you become still. Perhaps later, when you have trained yourself in meditation, you can feel yourself rise as on a shaft of light at this time. You then have power to function on a plane superior to this one and, looking down upon your emotional disturbance, you will see it for what it really is.

This control over emotion, anger and fear is one of the earliest degrees of initiation. It is achieved not by repression but by sublimation of these emotions, which can be seen by the clairvoyant as tongues of flame darting through the aura. All such things can be subdued and transmuted by the Christ within, and any passion that has been aroused, instead of injuring and destroying—for it *can* destroy—goes forth instead with power to heal, to bless, to lighten the burdens of the world, manifesting amid the darkness as pure white light.

Yes, it is said that one of the greatest barriers for a soul on the path is to overcome violent emotion, by which we mean to transmute it. Let it come out, but let it come out in love and as a cool, peaceful, harmonious vibration.

Beautiful Road Home

SEEK *and ye shall find.* The Master did not speak idly. The soul which seeks always finds. Sometimes the answer is found instantly. Sometimes a whole life may be lived before the answer comes;

but come it will, for there is always an answer to the search of the soul.

We know that it is not easy to extricate yourselves when you are immersed in the concerns of the material plane. We too have our limitations; for we too are bound to some extent, as you are, by the nature of our service and work. We were once asked why we came back into the heaviness of the earth conditions, having gained our freedom. We said in answer, 'Because we love our companions on earth; we are attracted to their need, and know we must come back to help them'. Thus we all have to suffer a degree of bondage; but because there is love in the heart, it sweetens all our work. This also applies to you; when you feel love in your heart, you are calm and at peace and all rebellion leaves you.

We have often told you that love is the first requisite. Your scriptures say that you may have many gifts, but if you lack love you are 'as sounding brass or a tinkling cymbal'. Love is the key. When you feel love towards life, love towards the beauty of the earth and all God's creation, you are filled with joy and even ecstasy, and the smallest thing can bring you the deepest happiness. Moreover, as soon as you love, you long to give. It is perhaps an unconscious desire, but always when you love, you give.

All the World Needs Healing

ALL THE world needs healing, and the great healer of all is love. By your love for each other, for all humankind, for the animal kingdom, for the world

Others

of nature, for God, you help in the salvation of this planet. The greater your love, the greater your power to help. So many organizations on earth seek to help in the cause of peace and progress, and all these organizations have their place, for they appeal to the varying mentality of men and women. But there is one common denominator—all souls will respond to love. It is so simple, so simple that some may get tired of hearing the words, *Love one another*.... The kingdom of heaven is within. But this is all, it is the completeness of life—to love, to be love, to become at one with love, to become part of the whole of love. Love radiates light, it heals, it comforts. But it is through constant life and work that this will take place. If you have love in your heart, you are doing God's work. You are God's instruments. Never forget a positive, constructive, unshakable thought of God.... God in everything, God everywhere—God Who has power to restore, to heal and to comfort humankind. We would convey to your hearts the truth of the power of love; but this you can prove for yourselves if you will put into operation the law of love in your own life.

L OVE IS the solvent of all difficulties, all problems, all misunderstandings. Apply love, by your inner attitude towards any human problem. Put aside the reasoning mind. Let divine love operate in you. From your inner self give God's love, and you will be surprised to find that every problem will be solved, every knot loosened.

THE QUIET MIND

9. Composure

THINK, speak, and act in the Light. Reach towards the Light, remembering that you can be a reflector of that Light.

A S WE look into your loving hearts, we see all the little weaknesses falling away, and only see that flame, that Divine Light which is in the heart of your soul. This is what the angels, the heavenly angels, see.

WHITE EAGLE'S LITTLE BOOK OF HEALING COMFORT

L OOK up to the sun-capped mountain range, the golden city—call it the kingdom of heaven if you like! But remember that the kingdom of heaven is not really a far country, the kingdom of heaven is found within yourself. You can make it a far country, or it can become close, a world of infinite beauty within yourself. People find it such a temptation, so much easier, to go here, there, everywhere, rushing to all kinds of places—to the east, to the west, to the north, to the south, in search of a master—and all the time the Master is within, so close. Nearer than breathing, closer than hands and feet. This is simple truth.

HEALING THE WORLD

The Best of White Eagle

Simplicity

PEOPLE make their lives so complex; they bring upon themselves an avalanche of confusion, pain and suffering; they are driven by desires of the mind and of the body, both of which enslave them. Yet the way to freedom is simple, so simple that most pass it by. Learn to listen to the voice of the Master within. So often men and women will not listen to the still voice of their Master, or they cannot recognize his voice. Or sometimes what they think to be the voice of their Master is only the voice of self, and self expresses itself in many ways—self-importance, self-love, wishing to shine before others. All these are of the lower self. But the voice of the Master within does not indulge in these emotions; it is gentle, selfless, at peace—at peace because it knows God.

Resignation

ALWAYS think in terms of the eternal Light. When things are not easy in your life, resign all in humility to the Light. As you attune yourself to the Light, so all good will come to you and in your life. Thus are you freed for ever from the limitations of physical matter.

In the heights, in the mountain tops, there live tranquillity and peace—which is the power, the wisdom and the love behind all human life; and in the depths of your heart lies the same tranquillity which is the power, the wisdom and the love of your life. Do not forget to turn to that inner light for your

Composure

succour and guidance. In that inner light you may meet the Brethren who work behind the scenes of the material life to send forth the light of the Star to suffering humanity. They—the Brethren—never doubt, they never look on the dark side; for they are Brethren, and they live in the Light and work with the Light—they are the Light. Follow their example and teaching. Do not allow yourselves to think, still less to utter words of fear, doubt, or failure. Think, speak, and act in the Light, with the Light, confident that the new world will be built according to the plan of the Great White Brotherhood so long as the builders or masons are true.

Every Sister and Brother of the Star knows that all is working for good, and that the Light absorbs the darkness everywhere.

Full of Light

YOU CAME from God, and to God you return. The spirit of each man or woman is as a 'little light', a little spark of life which came from the sun, not the sun you see in your sky, but the eternal universal sun, the sun behind the sun. We are all as tiny flames, breathed forth from that sun, and during the process of evolution this 'little light' grows, and becomes, at length, a blazing sun-star, a Christ.

Thus as the soul proceeds along the path, the light grows brighter; but not until it has travelled a long, long journey does this light within start to spread and radiate outside the form enclosing it. Picture a dark room, with a night-light burning in it. Such is the appearance of the one in whom the light has not yet grown bright and strong. Those who watch over humankind, looking for those likely to be of service, the Silent Watchers of humanity, can see immediately when the light is strong enough to lead, to guide others, and when that light can be used, can be stimulated and fanned into a fire. By the light within is each known to his or her teacher and master.

Will you, on the other hand, imagine a house illumined throughout, with every window open, and the light streaming forth across the quiet countryside; or maybe, across the great city within which it is placed? Compare the two: the first, the little chamber with the tiny light, barely visible; and on the other hand the house which is a blaze of light and warmth, a beacon shining across the countryside, or casting a great light in the city. This is the huge difference between a young soul whose light is still hidden, and the elder soul, casting the rays of spiritual light far and wide.

To God we return…! God is the light within; we are returning to God, grown in God's likeness, sons and daughters of God, of the light. Each 'window' in the house is one of the sacred chakras, which gradually become stimulated and alight through many initiations of minor degree, and are brought at last to full power and full radiance by the major initiations, by spiritual experience, spiritual illumination.

The Altar Within

YOU HAVE heard us say before that the human body can be likened to a temple. Within this temple is an altar on which burns a bright clear

Composure

flame. In your meditation seek this altar; try to imagine it, and bow your head in surrender before that altar flame within your temple. You yourself are creating this glowing altar and the light upon it. It is real, for it is being generated by you, is arising in you; and thus you see it in the form of an altar blazing with light. This is not your imagination; it is what you are actually creating by your aspiration, by your will, by concentration and direction of your thought. The flame which you see upon the altar may take the form of a rose with a brilliant jewel of light shining at its centre. If you see this in your meditation, remember that you are gazing upon your own heart centre. Or it may take the form of a pure white lotus with its many petals—again your own unfolding inner self. The chakras, instead of being closed and dull, are opening like flowers in the sunlight because of your meditation and aspiration.

The Temple

TO FIND truth you must experience it in your soul. You can read hundreds of books, or study the religions of all time, and find that all of them have one common point, one common denominator: and this is *love*—which is another word for light or soul-illumination. To realize this soul-illumination, you have to shut away the clamour of the lower mind, to become humble, very simple. Shall we try to explain it more clearly? Then imagine that you come into a temple to worship God. Now God is *in* you but God is also *outside* you. God is speaking to you both through nature and through your fellow beings, and in your inmost spirit. Through every experience, everything that happens in your life, God is speaking to you. God is your teacher, so think of God as being in your heart, God is actually *here* within your heart. In other words, the higher aspect of you is God.

Of course all life comes forth from God; darkness and light are both alike to God; the whole of creation is of God. We do want you to understand that you yourself are also a part of God, that God is speaking in you; so whenever you enter a temple of worship, even this small sanctuary, in your imagination, you can kneel before an altar of light, and in silence wait for God to speak.

How will God speak to you? In a 'feeling' that will come to you, a feeling of worship. As you kneel before that altar you worship, you thank God ... for life, for your friends, for your happiness, for sunshine and rain, for flowers and birds and animals, and for all the wonderful inventions making life easier and happier. Oh, the wealth of gifts that you could thank God for! Not least of your thankfulness should be for the companionship of your fellow creatures, for all those who have been instruments of God to bless your life. If you will only think back you will find there are great numbers of people whom you should thank. So, as you kneel before that altar, you will be pouring out blessing—for thankfulness is blessing. To feel truly thankful brings the outpouring of blessing upon life, even blessing upon God.

To be sure that what you learn from listening to our talks is true you must ask yourself, do you feel *instinctively* that it is truth? Yes, your spirit does feel

Com-
posure

thus impressed; but your earthly mind, mostly concerned with the activities of physical life, questions your spirit. As all wise people will tell you, that mind can be the slayer of truth. When that mind starts to analyze in a critical way, it is demolishing truths which by itself it can never restore. The mind demolishes; but the spirit of truth that is within will never lie, will never mislead you—*never*.

Therefore, whenever you feel that you want guidance, put aside all thoughts of self, or what *you* think you want. Don't allow your own desires to interfere with that pure light of God that can flow direct into your heart. What your heart tells you is truth is true indeed. To arrive at truth you must become very humble, very simple in yourself. The great people are those who are simple in heart. *I come in simple ways, in lowly ways, saith the Lord.*

Now, my children, life is ruled by law, and whatever you do brings a result. Even what you think sows a seed in you that grows. If it is not a good thought it will depress you; if it is a good thought, a hopeful thought, a God-thought, it will expand and bring you joy. The brethren in the world of spirit are exceedingly happy because they are peaceful in their hearts, undisturbed by dark happenings. You will say, 'Is it right to be undisturbed by the dark things?'. And we reply, 'Yes, my child, because by maintaining inner peace and letting the light burn steadily within you, you are doing far more good to your fellow creatures and to the world than if you get excited and argumentative with other people about disagreeable conditions'. Keep your poise. Be steady on your path.

A Still Lake

IF YOU would find an answer to every personal or world problem, practise the art of becoming very still within—as still and silent as the surface of a lake without a breath of wind to disturb it. This lake represents your soul, and when it is still and you have developed the will of God within yourself, then you will see without distortion the reflection of truth on the waters of the lake which is your soul or 'psyche'. 'Be still, and know that I am God'. When a soul is alone with God, God speaks to it. The individual then sees truth reflected in his or her own psyche. But if the person does not use the *divine* will, does not pray for the will of God to be done; if people are wilful, seeking an answer in accord with their own desires, then the answer will be distorted, for there is no peace in any of them, the lake of their souls is not still.

The soul of each man and woman is a wonderful instrument, and can be likened to a radio receiver with which the person can tune in to many stations, either to spheres in the grey lower astral worlds of disquiet and desire, or to spheres where all life is a manifestation of the beauty of God; and even, if the person so desires, to other planets of the solar system. The human being has indeed been given wings, but has yet to learn how to unfold these wings and rise into worlds of infinite beauty.

In your prayers and aspirations, you may touch a vibration of purity that you feel in your heart as simple goodness. Such a pure feeling as this does not depend upon possession of a powerful and well-stored mind, but upon a pure and constant joy uprising in the heart. Every son or daughter of the living God should live joyfully. If you analyze our words, you will find they are profoundly true. Take as an example your own life. If you were touching the secret of joy, and recognized and faithfully cherished in your life this pure joy in God, how different your feelings and outlook would be!

Think of the immense blessing conferred upon humankind by the soul who can live in joy and pure goodness without any thought of the result to self. The ideal, of course, is to do right because you love the right, because the joy within you, the life of the spirit within you, cannot do other than express itself as goodness.

Have you ever thought that only the goodness of individual men and women safeguards the future of the race? If there were no goodness in the world, there would be no future for humanity. The man or woman who lives in singleness of purpose to do good, to be good, to live happily, makes an enormous gift to generations yet unborn. Nevertheless, we recognize that it is not easy to do good, or even to be good yourself just for the sake of goodness alone. Please believe that we do not preach at you; we are only trying to work out a certain theme which we can presently make clearer. Again and again, we say that if you can establish a foundation of joy and serenity within yourself, and express goodness in every action and in life itself, your contribution to the happiness of humankind will be beyond your power to estimate.

This can be illustrated by the life of Jesus. If you could only learn about that life in more detail, grasping its simplicity and humility; if you could realize his continual outpouring of the magical white light of heaven to help and heal, you would understand that only joy and goodness can truly release this power of the white magic. Any similar life is by its very nature continually pouring forth a divine essence.

This fact has been demonstrated by other great teachers. The yogis of the East have also discovered the source of all true happiness and the secret of a richer life. The continual service they pour forth to humankind does not seem like labour to them. Rather is it a spontaneous and constant outpouring of divine essence.

Your Calling

REMEMBER always the quiet, pure and true contact within the sanctuary of your own being. Be true to your own self, your own spirit, and in being true to yourself you will be true also to God and the universal Brotherhood.

Many people on earth and many sources on the etheric plane will delight in trying to pull you away from that still centre of truth. Do not be pulled; but hold fast to the pure vision of goodness, truth and love. Be watchful and alert and do not be beguiled by false values. It is easy to slip off the straight path.

Having offered yourselves in sincerity and faith to the work of God and the Brotherhood, remember that *the starting point of this work is yourself.* We can only give you principles or signposts and you must work in the simplest way on each problem as it presents itself to you in your daily life, according to the

SPIRITUAL UNFOLD- MENT IV

Com- posure

121

principles given you. We do not come to relieve you of your opportunities. We come to bring you power, wisdom and love. We of the Brotherhood do not expect more than you can give at your present stage on the path, but everyone can, at given times, seek attunement with the Eternal Light, can commune with God, can worship God. This you do in ways most harmonious to you personally. There are many rays reaching from the periphery to the centre, but whichever ray your soul is on, reach forward to God, the heart from which the lifeblood flows. The Brethren in the Temple sit in a circle, hand in hand, their hearts reaching out to the heart in the centre. This is truly the round table of the Knights of the Temple. You are all striving to become true knights.

Your Master teaches you in a very simple way the rules of the Brotherhood and you must endeavour to understand and apply these rules to your life.

KEEP your feet on the earth but lift your face towards the heavens, for the light that floods into you from on high will steady your feet and guide them in the right path. Have confidence in this divine light. Surrender with a tranquil mind and a heart full of love to this infinite wisdom.

THE QUIET MIND

10. Mastery

EACH time your eyes are opened to the right way of life, each time you are able to touch the secret inner life, life takes on a new aspect.

THE MASTER is nearer than breathing, closer than hands and feet. This is simple truth. You will find nothing more beautiful than what you can find in your own inner temple. You will find there the greatest treasure, the perfect gift.

TREASURES OF THE MASTER WITHIN

YOU ARE never truly alone; the companion of your spirit, your beloved, is with you all the time. You are only lonely if you isolate yourself in your physical life and consciousness. Your spirit can rise above this limitation and join your loved ones. But this means continual effort, an awakening of that inward knowing that you call 'faith'. You must have faith in God's love.

LIVING WITH LOVE

All-Enfolding Love

W E COME into your midst bringing a love which we find inexpressible in words. We only pray that the Great Spirit of love will use us as instruments to convey to you a realization of the all-enfolding love and protection of God, of which you stand in so much need. We are speaking to you collectively but also individually, because we are aware of your fears, your anxieties, and of your heart's hunger. Would that we could raise you from the earth-bound consciousness that so often imprisons you.

Never think that we cannot enter into your troubles, or understand the weariness of the body and the anxiety of the mind. Never think that we are unconcerned by your mental or material troubles. Every secret of your souls is known to the masters. They work as with one mind, in complete unison, but when they descend to the level of humanity each has his own particular branch of work. Yet at the highest all masters are *one*. This is because the master mind is in complete attunement with the universal mind, where truth abides. Radiations of truth go forth from this centre to envelop the whole universe and every individual life.

The angels and the Christ himself are not so remote as you are apt to think. You have the power—even at this very moment!—to leave all to follow him, so that you can abide with him in his high estate. Try to remember this, more particularly when you are bowed down by material troubles, and cares; for it is then that he calls, saying, *Leave all and follow me … for I AM the way, the truth and the life.*

Men and women make such a mistake when they think of heaven as removed, as far beyond their attainment. Heaven is within every one of you, and you must learn to find heaven while you are still in a physical body. Then you will surely migrate to a heavenly plane, when you slip off your coat of skin at physical death.

You are Never Alone

WHILE no soul is left in isolation, yet every soul must pass through its initiation alone. Every soul must also pass from one state of life to another alone. It is this very aloneness, this mist that shrouds the future, which eventually forces the soul to progress.

At first, the soul is like a child thinking it is self-sufficient, believing itself able to accomplish anything and everything, capable of solving on its own the puzzle of living. Through loneliness, it discovers the true Source of its strength. Indeed, on occasion that soul will specially need to be alone; for when the long-blinded eyes at last open and the soul's expansion or quickening takes place, it must be in solitude. This may happen to you: perhaps in this period of bondage you are purposely being left to yourself in order to develop your inner strength and faith in God.

What is this faith? Faith is an inner knowing that God can never fail in goodness and love. Every soul must develop this faith in God: not only this inner knowing that God is good, but also faith in the God within itself. Encased as you are in materialism, you are very easily misguided. It is as if a descending shutter had blacked out your awareness of the spiritual life about you. That is why earthly matters seem to you far more important than heavenly. Your real self is battened down in the hold of your own ship of life. That ship is your soul, which is being tossed hither and thither on the sea of emotion until in your extremity you cry out to awaken the master of the ship, the Christ. On the instant, he arises and says, 'Peace, be still!'—and the turbulent emotions subside and all is peace.

We are with You

IF YOU will be steadfast on the path to which your feet have been guided—by brethren before you on that path—you will find the treasure of life, a never-ending stream of help and healing and happiness. We, your brothers and guides, are on the road by your side. Not one of you stands alone. You have only to ask in simple trust, and you shall receive; whatever your need, it shall be supplied. Each one of you has your own guide by your side, one who never leaves you. Your guide knows your innermost need and will comfort you and lead you into green pastures and beside still waters.

Some of you are faced with problems that seem to be insurmountable, and you may think that we in spirit know nothing of your own human needs and your difficulties. You do not realize how close we are, or that sometimes when you are out of your body, in your sleep, you come to us and confide your weakness, your worry, your sorrow. Your brethren over here understand and are waiting to help you.

Mastery

Do you know that many of these friends are around you now, acting as silent helpers, silent watchers, ever on the lookout for opportunities to serve and to help, to guide and to inspire you?

We who come from the inner world are well aware of the practical details of human life. You may think that being spirit we are quite remote from the activities and the pains and the fears and the sufferings of our brothers and sisters on earth, but here you would be very much mistaken. The Brotherhood of the White Light is closely concerned with the evolution, happiness and wellbeing of all humanity. We have passed through many incarnations and have the means of recalling these human experiences when necessary. Therefore we can feel with you; we can understand your frustrations, your limitations and your anxieties and fears. We can understand physical pain and spiritual suffering. We are part of you; we are one of you; we are with all of you.

We Understand your Difficulties

We who have left behind us the bondage of earthly bodies understand the difficulties that confront our brothers and sisters in the physical life. You know the saying that 'the stones that cut the pupil's feet have first wounded the Master'? He has walked the selfsame path, and his feet have been cut also. We are so attuned to you, our brethren, that we absorb your feelings.

We do not speak in loud language of the things of the spirit. It is better not to shout from the hilltops, and so we just keep quietly on, you with us, and we with you. We are not unmindful of your grief, your anxieties, your disappointments. We share all these with you; but we can see beyond your vision, and the way we help you is by coming back from the spirit life to bring you hope and light. This we shall always do.

We know that every grumble, every depressing, fearful thought, can weave greyness and darkness into your spirit—which should be a radiant thing. You may wonder why sometimes you find it practically impossible to realize the presence of spiritual beings; and at others you feel so sure of the presence of your guide. Why is it that on certain days you feel blank and heavy? At another time you feel as if on a mountain-top, with clean bright air about you. You get distinct impressions from the spirit world; you feel so sure of your guide, and that everything is going to be all right. When they arise, the density and heaviness you experience are there because you are literally in a psychic fog—compared to the higher, spiritual sunlight you otherwise find. At such periods, cling with all your strength to the consciousness that the sun is there behind the mists: your helpers are still closely with you.

We know the sorrows of human existence because we have ourselves endured them. We know the heartaches, the disappointments of human life, its fears and doubts and terrors. We know also that behind the whole of human endeavour there is hope and light, kindled out of humanity's persistent thoughts of kindliness and goodwill. While we are here with you on earth we participate in your life, your thoughts, your sorrows—but we do not take them with us when we rise into the spirit realms. Instead, we bring happiness and love down to you.

You are not shut away from this glorious

Brotherhood that we describe to you, or only insofar as you shut yourself away. You can close around you a barrier of despair and darkness and fear, and then you separate yourself from this Brotherhood, for the Brotherhood will never intrude upon your wish for isolation. But if you open your heart and say 'come' they come, so joyously, and will never fail to do so. We see, not the outer shell, but the beloved spirit, our true brother and sister, within the shell; it is because we can see this that we love you and do not see the mists, which are but the physical coverings.

Find Good in the Silence
This we advise you to do: seek in the silence to discover the beautiful jewel in your brethren. Love one another and see good in all men and women, deep within—see the jewel within the lotus. This will help you to keep your contact with the Brotherhood in the world of spirit. By this we do not mean only the exalted beings, but all those kindly, sincere, loving friends who are yours on the spirit planes of life.

So we of the Brotherhood come to lift you into the world of light and to help you to live, in thought, in our world of spirit. We are able to draw close to you at all times. We want you to realize this and call to us and speak to us on the inner planes. We will never fail to answer you, but you need first a greater faith and trust, and to disentangle yourselves from the doubts and fears of earth life. You *want* to believe, but you are not always strong enough. So we urge you to be true in your friendship and your love for these silent helpers. If the light of the Star shines from your heart, you open the way for shining brothers and sisters from the world of spirit to draw close and lead you through the doorway into the realms of light and truth. You are all like young plants with roots in the dark earth, and are struggling to send green shoots above the earth, and some flowers and blossoms. This is the purpose of everyday life, but it does need effort: effort from the spirit within you.

We want you to come up as often as you can into this sphere of harmony and truth, so that you become immersed in it—just as a sponge, immersed, becomes full of water. You will become full of the light and harmony of those higher spheres, and then the darkness will have no power over you.

The brothers in the spirit world can and will help you to solve every difficulty; for when you surrender yourselves and your life into the wise and loving keeping of your Father–Mother God, you break down the barrier that material thought has created, and the help you need flows to you. So, when you are perplexed and fearful, will you think of your brethren of the Lodge above, who, through the instrument of the golden Star, pour streams of golden light into the soul to awaken the Christ in you? Surrender, yield yourselves up to the golden light, and let it pour through every fibre of your being. Let it dissolve every disappointment and difficulty. Each time your eyes are opened to the right way of life, each time you are able to touch the secret inner life, the light expands in your heart and soul. Then life takes on a new aspect. You see with eyes both spiritual and physical a lovelier vista, a more profound beauty than you have seen before—and your heart will sing with praise and thanksgiving to your Creator.

A S STUDENTS of our words, you are part of a company of brethren who are all seeking the light of the spirit, and you are aided by those illumined brethren who come back to help you in your search. They are the hidden companions of your journey. They know you, although you may not know them in your physical consciousness. They are the companions whom you meet when you enter into a state of meditation, when you are withdrawn from the world, or when you leave your physical body at the time of sleep. Later on at death you will meet these beloved ones, for they are your true companions and the spiritual life is your real life. You have stepped down from a land of light into darkness. You have donned something like a diver's suit for this purpose, descending into the depths to search for treasure, for the pearl of great price. It is wise to get a truer perspective of life, unwise to think of mortal life as all-important, although it has its significance, of course.

Each time we speak to you, we have to remind you of the company of shining angelic ones who are with us. We do this because we understand the heaviness of the flesh and earthly mind. Some people living forget or do not know that they have many unseen friends, relatives and companions. They naturally think of people about them as being the only ones who know them, the only people whom they know. They forget—indeed they do not know— that they have lived through many, many ages and in the course of their long journey through matter they have met, lived with, and enjoyed the friendship of many, many souls. So bear this in mind: that you have around you beloved companions, some of whom you know, and a number you do not. In the course of your spiritual unfoldment you will hold communion with these friends unseen.

This should be a source of comfort to those of you who feel lonely, particularly those who live in a family that cannot share your interests. If you are in such condition, remember you are there by your own choice and for a purpose; and that you have in spirit your true family, who are people in perfect harmony with your spirit, and who help you to live your life nobly, wisely, profitably. These invisible brethren are souls with whom you have lived in past incarnations and with whom you have a great bond of sympathy and love. It is also true that in your present life you are sometimes brought into contact with people with whom you instantly feel at home. Then you know instinctively that they too are very old friends or former relatives. Beyond these, there are souls with whom you are brought into close and intimate relationship, yet with whom you feel you have nothing in common—yet you know that there must be a link of some kind. Therefore think of yourself as having a very large company of friends moving along the path of life with you. However alone you may appear, yet you are not alone. Quite the reverse!

Guidance

THERE IS such a thing as spiritual guidance, not only through the innermost being, not only through the inner light, but guidance by guides, wise

friends, or guardian angels in the beyond. The spirit
guide helps because the guide has a clearer vision
than either the healer or the patient; the guide can
inspire and tell the healer what method a particular
patient requires. The guide can help the healer by directing the hands, by directing the rays, and also by
talking to the subconscious of the patient. Yes, the
guide does a lot of work in healing, in collaboration
with the healer and the patient!

Many are responding unconsciously to such guidance. The time will come when all of you will respond to your guardian angel. By then, humans and
angels will walk side by side on earth. *Ask, and it shall
be given you*—ask for guidance, particularly as you fall
asleep at night, and be on the alert for impressions
in the early morning. Answers will be dropped into
your minds. You will be amazed at the true guidance and help forthcoming. In time, your guide will
become known to you as a very much loved companion. Every one has a guide, but not every one has
open eyes, nor open ears.

*WE RAISE our hearts in prayer and thanksgiving
for life, for the wondrous love and wisdom
which guides our lives. Eternal Spirit, our hearts pray
that [we] may be caught up in the power and the light
of the glory; that each may hear the singing of angels
and feel the brush of their wings. May the inner vision
open for all our companions here assembled; and may
the lotus cup of communion be filled to overflowing
with thy Spirit.*

PRAYER, MINDFULNESS AND INNER CHANGE

11. Reunion

WHAT you call death is more truly an initiation.

NEVER fear your journey ahead, for as God has watched over you all your life and, in spite of your fears, has brought you through all the trials and sorrows of your life, so God will take you through the darkest vale, into the light.

TRY TO regard the physical body only as the clothing of the soul, the outer coat. When you have reached to the centre, to the truth that is God, spirit, you will only be conscious of eternally living and will not be separated at any time from those you love and have loved. In that state of cosmic consciousness you are united with all you love, for in love there is no separation. If you who are listening to these words have lost dear companions by the release of the spirit, if you have lost the physical form, we advise you to use your thought power and create in your minds, see your loved ones. Think of them, speak to them spirit to spirit. This takes a little time for you to understand, but if you persevere in your quiet moments in thinking of the spirit world as always there, always being brought into vision and manifestation, you will eventually live in that consciousness of life, not in all its drabness and suffering and restriction as in a physical body, but a life in which the spirit is free as the lark in the sky.

The World of Light

WE COME to you to help you to expand your consciousness to that world of light, which is interpenetrating your physical world. It is a great mistake to separate the levels of life by saying, 'we are down here on the earth', and 'the spirit world or heaven is up there'. We want you all to grow in the consciousness of this interpenetration of the higher worlds. We say 'higher worlds' not because they are set apart from you, but yet they are light worlds: they are not to be found in the dense material consciousness. They are instantly to be found when you open yourself in love. Your thoughts of love never fail to reach those you love who have passed onward. If you truly love your companion he or she is with you, closer than breathing, because both of you are part of God. You can never be separated from those you love, so long as you love them, and you love God; you are all one.

WHITE EAGLE'S LITTLE BOOK OF COMFORT FOR THE BEREAVED

Many Mansions

ESTABLISH in your mind that human life is essentially infinite and eternal; that there has never been a time when you were not, and there never will be. At this, you will ask, 'Shall we not get tired of this ceaseless round of incarnation? Even now, life is a burden!'. This is why God has limited your days in the flesh; you live on earth only for a few short years which you call an incarnation, and then you leave your body as an outworn dress, and go for refreshment to your true home in the spirit.

In daily life, you do not mind moving from one house to another; you may love your old house, but

FIRST STEPS ON A SPRITUAL PATH

Reunion

when you have had enough of it you are ready to go. So also you come to the point when you would like a new body; you are weary and tired of the old. Then God is kind and allows you to pass on. You are removed from an outgrown state of existence and move onward to the next state.

Once over there, finding a measure of freedom such as you had never before experienced, you can rise in spirit to enter upon a period of intense happiness far removed from the former ignorance and limitation of your earth life. Then, when you have rested sufficiently and have assimilated the lessons of your earth life, your interest in incarnation is quickened, and the time comes for you to go forth again.

Let us make it quite clear: you need never be separated from your loved ones. Where there is love there can be no separation. Love attracts love as a magnet attracts steel, and you are inevitably drawn to loved ones, both in the spirit and as you go forth to fresh incarnation. The same law operates in all worlds.

Truly, *eye hath not seen nor ear heard* the glories prepared by God for the child of God. Humanity's limited consciousness has as yet no power to comprehend these glories. Men and women cannot even realize the vast range of varied existence in the animal and human kingdom, let alone the subtler etheric, astral, mental or celestial planes which encircle and interpenetrate the earth and will be their future homes.

Emerging from Darkness

EVERY one of you here has, at some time, been through an ordeal, something you dreaded—

perhaps an operation, perhaps giving birth to a child, or even the separation from a loved one. And although you have anticipated the worst, yet when the time came, a very gentle, sweet power came to you, and you were able to go through the feared ordeal with calmness, with a certain inner sweetness and love. So it is with death. Although the body may have to be discarded, the soul body is healed, and when it awakens after death, it is so well, so happy. However you pass away from your physical body, whether suddenly, by accident, or by a slow process of withdrawal, we would like you to understand that death is no dark vale, but rather it is a beautiful experience for the soul. Try to realize that you are not the physical body, any more than you are the clothes you wear. Your body is like the clothes you wear, and when the great transition comes to you, you will lay it aside as you lay aside your material clothing. But your true self, your invisible self, lies deep within you.

Indeed, what you call death is more truly an initiation of either lesser or greater degree for the human soul; and the culmination comes when the outer garment is committed to the fire. Then a great light breaks upon the soul. O children of earth, we beg you not to regard the passing of the soul from the body into immortal life as something to be dreaded! At the right time—for that time comes according to the law of God—the soul goes forth, not to lose its identity but to gain greater consciousness of God and awareness of the eternal light. Remember also when your friend is taken from you that the inner soul of man and woman knows the day and the time, the hour, when it has to leave this physical body. This may be an unconscious or a conscious knowledge, but the hour of passing cannot be altered by humanity, only by the Law of God. You must accept the loving wisdom of God and send the soul forth joyously, with your love and blessing, into that larger, happier, freer life. You must do this.

Lastly, remember that love disperses all mists. At the moment you may seem to be divided from those you love who have passed into the world of spirit. But you are not truly separated, although before you hangs a mist—sometimes a heavy fog. This fog is an individual's own creation. When he or she has light and love in the heart it warms and so shines through and disperses the mist. Then that man or woman sees clearly into the worlds of higher ethers. There she sees her loved ones; he sees life as a whole. It is not a question of humankind being 'here' and the spirit 'over there' with a closed door between the two. Understanding reveals that life is universal, that the life of the spirit is identical with life on earth. True, the spirit world is a world more beautiful than this, but then it is made beautiful by the love which a soul learns to operate once it is away from the limitations with which it binds itself in the flesh.

Beloved, have you lost ones dear to you? Think of them, then, as in the sunlight of the worlds beyond, absorbing the very essence of the spirit. There is no death: progress ... progress ... growth ... a life-force ever moving onward, forward into the Sun.

The Life Abundant

WE ARE now especially speaking to those who have lost someone near and dear to them. We say that they are just the same as when you formerly

knew and loved them. They are the same person-
alities; they are still your own father or son, brother
or sister, husband or wife. They are just the same,
only so much happier because they are freed from
the cares, distress and confusion of earth. Their joy
increases when they feel you are attuned to them in
your soul, and that you believe and know that they
are close. Try to talk to them within your soul body,
mentally, and make them real to you.

We tell you with tenderness that you bring much
of your suffering upon yourselves. You will ask how
we can say this when, for instance, your hearts are
sore through bereavement. No, of course you did
not bring bereavement upon yourself—only the suffering which resulted from your attitude of mind. For
if you had developed power to penetrate the mists of
earthliness, you would have known that your dear
one was not dead or far away. Communion of soul
with soul is always waiting for the man or woman
who can develop, within, a consciousness of the one-
ness of all life. Learn so to love God that you know
that God, being all love, and having all love for you,
has in Him–Her no death, but only a more abundant
life. Your loved one dwells within that Love, and also
within your own spirit. Your loved one is therefore
with you, not lost, not gone far away.

Try never to think of anyone as being 'dead'.
Think of them as living more abundantly in a land
which you know they would love—and please, not
as living idly; idleness they would not find inspiring.
Wherever their heart inclines them they will find
their work, and work to their heart's content.

Believe that all the experiences of your daily life

Reunion

come to discipline and to teach you, even if they are sometimes painful; for joy only comes about through pain. The wise person knows that even when apparent tragedy brings bereavement to a family, it is presently revealed to them that a wise purpose has been served, in that the passing brought an eventual fulfilment to many people.

The wise one never grieves over the dead or over the living, because he or she knows that God in His–Her wisdom and compassion cares for and succours all earthly creatures. How can we ever find adequate words truly to convey to the anxious human heart the rich love, the transcendent beauty, and the enduring peace of God?

They Come with Shining Faces

WHITE
EAGLE'S
LITTLE
BOOK OF
COMFORT
FOR THE
BEREAVED

WHEN you have lost a loved one, may we remind you to recognize that it is only the physical body, like an outworn coat that has lost its usefulness, that you are missing. Hold fast to the truth that spirit is eternal, and that the personality, the beloved personality, is always there. Life changes, the scenes of life change; but the basic, the essential life of a person, the nature of the individual, is eternal. You have also been given the qualities within yourself and the power, the gifts of the psyche, which enable you to make contact with spirit at will, and with the spirit of your loved ones.

You have only to think of your loved one to bring him or her close. Not careworn, not suffering; don't think of the pain and the distortion of the countenance during years of suffering. Think of your loved one with a face—a face like a shining Master, like Jesus or like Buddha, or any one of the great teachers. Think of him or her in that world of light. And remember that when you are there in meditation, or maybe in a dream, you will notice how happy they look. How smooth and beautiful then is the face of your loved one, showing quite clearly the feelings that are peaceful, joyous and thankful!

They bless you, they love you, and they want you to know that life for them has not ceased, but that they continue to live in a happier and freer condition. If you could only be there in the garden of reunion and remembrance you would know that there is no death. The separation is one that you, with your material minds, create. Your dear one is close beside you now. What you think habitually you become. If you habitually think along the lines of goodwill, of good thought, God thought, you draw nearer every day to your companions who dwell in the light.

These dear ones who are with you are also living in that state of harmony you call heaven, because they have heard the voice of goodness, of God. We wish you could see the happiness with which these people work in their own particular section in the spirit world. Each one is drawn, as by a magnet, to the very sphere and to the particular work that their soul most enjoys. Whatever the interest of your loved one, that interest is given to them in their life in spirit. Your loved ones are happy, and they rejoice in their service.

They come close to you and they whisper in your heart. Or, if you are trained in meditation and are able to release yourself from the burden and darkness of the earthly mind—so that you are able to enter the garden of remembrance in the spirit world—then your loved ones immediately come to you. It is the spiritual law of attraction. They come to you if you can imagine with your higher vision that you are with them. It is these inner powers and qualities of the spirit that you have to develop—so that you are always aware, conscious, of the companionship of your beloved ones, because in spirit there is no separation.

*A*T DEATH *there is physical separation, but no separation of the human spirit which is the real self. If you truly love your companion he or she is with you, closer than breathing, because both of you are part of God.*

LIVING WITH LOVE

*B*EHOLD *now a cloud of unseen witnesses are with you. See the radiant forms around you, see the forms of the angels, and personal loved ones draw close and become at one with you. Behold there is no separation in God's universe. You are in God, and God is in you. Your guide is in you, is part of you, and you are part of your guide, there is no separation. All are of God, and there is no separation in God. You are in God, and God is perfect.*

PRACTISING PEACE

12. Truth

EVERY soul at some time must make its stand for truth, must stand forth as a warrior, and fight for what it knows to be right and true.

IT IS rightly said that there is no new truth. We would add that all truth is contained within God. God is within you, but at present in you only as a seed, a seed-atom. But with the advance of humanity this seed will commence to grow, and you will find a dawning heavenly life, not in some far-off place but within your own temple, within your heart.

WHITE EAGLE ON THE INTUITION AND INITIATION

A Simple Approach

THE FUNDAMENTAL purpose of your life is that you may find truth, truth which will be unveiled to you by your own inner self. As we search for this truth which lies buried deep within, the barriers erected by the outer self will vanish and we shall become free, free to hold communion with those we love in the beyond, free to contact the cosmic rays of life-force and healing; free to use them in the service of others; free to become *en rapport* with those beings who minister to humanity from the spirit.

The pathway which climbs the mountainside to the heavenly summit is long and steep; and until men and women obtain a glimpse of the glory which awaits them, they are in travail on the planes of materialism. They suffer pain, sickness, isolation, limitation; they remain heirs to fear, resentment, anxiety, and are afflicted by conflicts and wars. But no one need wait until after they are freed from the flesh to realize their happiness and their true being. Indeed, unless men and women learn to seek the spirit while they are still on earth they will not find complete freedom or joy merely by discarding the physical body.

A glorious future awaits each soul, but it entails hard work—although even hard work can be very interesting. For instance, if you love music and long to express yourself through music, it becomes a joy to practise, to acquire mastery over your instrument. If you are wholly interested in something worthwhile you do not mind taking pains, nor do you count the cost of attainment. So it should be with this work spent upon your soul.

Truth

The path which all must tread, leading to the temple of the soul, is the same. The outer mind—the normal thinking apparatus—must be slowed down. You cannot hope to contact the source of truth within if your mind is full of unimportant details of earthly life. This is where you have to learn discrimination, because earthly life makes so many claims: usually all the attention of the individual goes on its everyday needs. So many unimportant things assume great importance in the earthly mind, but if you can resolutely keep your attention upon what is taking place on the spiritual side of your life, and try to register impressions from the higher self, you will be able to overcome that insistent torturing of the earthly mind. We advise you not to make a point of suppressing the lower aspect of your life, but of encouraging the beautiful. We advise you to encourage the true spiritual expansion of your real self in daily contacts until it becomes a natural unfoldment, a natural development of that soul which has been living for countless years.

True to Yourself

WHITE
EAGLE ON
INTUITION
AND
INITIATION

*The Best
of White
Eagle*

THERE are paradoxes which you continually meet on the spiritual path. Sometimes, we know it feels as though at every step there is a paradox. It is so confusing that you do not know what is meant, or which path you should take. Here again people are liable to lay down hard-and-fast rules. One says 'We must go that way!'. Another says 'No, this is the path—I *know*'. What are you to do? You are faced with a deep spiritual problem, and you have eventually to learn by your intuition to discriminate between what are sometimes described as the upper and the lower, or the left-hand and the right-hand paths. Here you cannot be bound by another's advice, because what is right for him or her, what is his or her pathway, is not necessarily yours. You must decide for yourselves which is the way to journey.

Yes ... discrimination. *Everyone knows our duty but ourselves!* 'If I were you, Ms So and So, I should take this course.' *But would you?* If you were placed in exactly the vibrations, the conditions, and with the same qualities of soul-development, would you do as you say you would? How *can* anyone judge for another soul, whose quality of consciousness, whose feelings and reactions, are vastly different from their own? You cannot decide for anyone else, and no one else can decide for you. So, when these little arguments crop up, smile and say 'Yes ... I know'. Say nothing to hurt the person who is so eager to advise you. Do not say, 'Oh no, I know that is not my path, you are quite wrong!'. Say 'Yes....', but retain your inner knowing. And don't forget the smile!

Are we encouraging you to be deceptive? No. Men and women on earth need to wear masks at times. Yet they also need so to develop their 'x-ray vision' that they see through the mask to the real person beneath. When they can do this, they do not judge, they understand and have a feeling of goodwill and fellowship for everyone.

The Path to the Mysteries
As we bring through to the earth plane our knowledge or revelation to help humanity, we find it very

difficult to clothe inner truths in earthly language and pictures. We can convey a certain amount to you without words. We contact the halls of wisdom, and there is a line of communication down through the spheres, to an earth channel or instrument. But when our message comes right down into your midst, it has to come through an earthly vessel to an audience that is very limited—with apologies to you—but *of necessity* limited in its power to comprehend these inner secrets or mysteries of heaven. We in spirit are indeed handicapped by this.

Because we contact the halls of wisdom, the power of heaven comes with us; and those of you who are sensitive are able to catch a little of the light here and there. Your own vision opens; and although you yourself cannot put truth into words, you feel an inner knowing as you grasp these truths, these mysteries of God. This, of course, has always been the case, and as you read the Bible or any of the other great scriptures of the world, you will gradually uncover these age-old secrets. Yet until such secrets are uncovered, you will be left without an answer to many of your questions.

Today all people are free to follow the path, if they will, towards the mysteries. Some may speed and others loiter. Yet once you desire wisdom, not for your own satisfaction, not because of curiosity, but that you may labour to serve the whole earth, then your feet are placed on the path which leads ultimately to the house of light. And so, out of the great longing within your heart to serve, you find yourself. Once this happens, your soul is assisted with teaching, with guidance from the invisible. If you try and sample too many paths you will find each one of them leads to a cul-de-sac; we say therefore, you are better to abide on the one path. Follow the one path, giving service: follow the light and guidance from your invisible teachers, and then the mysteries of the invisible worlds will be revealed to you. There are many ways of serving, and no student is bound to follow the path set by others; you should follow the light which shines from your own spirit.

Remember, then, the very first indication of truth, of true teaching, is simplicity. Simplicity first, and then profundity. Call to mind the simple and yet profound revelation of the Master Jesus; and that of the Lord Buddha. Look, then, for simplicity first in all revelation. Then follow it diligently; put into practice the actual *being* ... being and becoming in very truth those beautiful truths which have been revealed. Don't seek for short-cuts into the temple. There can be no gate-crashing ... only a steady upward climb, during which many a test must be passed.

The particular training which took place in the temple of the olden days, the seclusion and isolation which enabled the student finally to graduate, is gone. Today your life must be spent in a workaday world. People in what you call developed society are not shielded from the temptation of the outer world. Rather, the student is subject to the continual pull of the lower world, of excitements and the passions of the physical life. In former days, he or she withdrew, quietly pursued the path, worked diligently, and gave healing to the sick and comfort to those who mourned. Powers came which enabled him or her to draw aside the veil between their world and the invisible worlds. These same powers can be yours today.

Truth

But you must literally go forth to the battlefield of life, and there learn to discriminate between the false and the true, between the real and the unreal. Oh, we know it! It is not easy!

Many of you on earth today were once workers in the Egyptian temples, particularly those of you who now serve in some simple and humble centre of spiritual light. Those drawn to such places have already learned certain inner truths which abide; because while the physical life passes, and even the personality brought onward from the past to a future life is dropped and hung up in the 'wardrobe' above (there to wait until required for use), the inner wisdom once learned from a mystery school is never lost. That is why many of you feel the stirring—the Ancient Wisdom—within your breast. You do not need to be convinced. Once you have seen into the invisible world, you *know*.

Meanwhile, we can only hint. We can only say things that will stir and quicken your minds and hearts so that you will catch a train of thought or intuition and follow that intuition. Spiritual truth is fluid. You can get principles upon which to work, but truth is like a great river with many tributaries. You will get sidetracked, and you may get lost, but always you will come back to the main theme, the main principle. If you can rise above the earth and look down, you will see where all the tributaries flow, see them all fit into the grand panorama of beautiful life on earth, the Garden of Eden.

We too have only caught a glimpse of the grandeur of the universe, only a brief insight into the possibilities which lie within all. But such knowledge as we have garnered in our meditations we give to you, as it may prove a signpost on your own journey—along your path of eternal progress and eternal unfoldment, leading to eternal light and glory.

The spiritual universe may indeed be beyond your comprehension, but from what we have seen of it, we can only tell you it is glorious, overwhelming and unbelievable to those who have yet to comprehend the love of God. To describe it any further is like trying to pour a great volume of liquid through a very small funnel. You see, what we have to say does not bring with it proof that the worldly mind accepts. The only proof of these spiritual truths is that by the way of life you live, you receive the proof and the demonstration of truth. To put it in very simple language: the truths work; and they work in the tiniest detail of your everyday life. You can all prove them for yourselves, but we cannot prove them for you. Any living man or woman can prove them if they like to apply the law to their daily lives. As they do so, they can see the glory of the heavens; they can realize the happiness of the spirit.

Spiritual Growth is the Result of Perseverance

IF YOU meet what you call failure, do not despair and say, 'I am not there yet'. The very fact that you are trying shows you are at one level already there. If not, you would not be trying. The fact that you can create a longing and set your vision on an ideal shows that you are ready.

Remember that when you are on this path the

graph goes up and down. The soul is bound to be carried up to the heights and bound to descend again. At times you will feel full of spiritual ecstasy and can do anything; and there will be times when you feel hopeless. Never, never mind. Hold on with a loving heart to your ideal and to your Father–Mother God, the Parents who are watching over you, who understand their child because they have given you birth. Keep on persevering with your everyday life and with your set lessons, thereby bringing this light within into conscious operation, so that the very cells of your body become finer. This is what is happening in the world. Spirit—God—is continually moulding, purifying, raising the world's vibrations.

Let us remember that only a part of the soul comes back with each incarnation, and not the greater self; what incarnates is only like a feeler, like an arm put forth to gather more experiences into the greater self. So, if you lack opportunity for certain lessons, it does not mean that you do not need those lessons, but that you have come back with a set purpose, and that the other lessons are not on your horizon for this particular incarnation. You are set to gain experience on one particular line. Whether you are developed on other lines, or whether your neighbour is developed on these lines or not, you cannot tell. How impossible it is for you to judge your companion! You do not know his or her soul; unwittingly, you may be entertaining a great being in your house! You do not know. Some people have peculiar ways of showing their greatness, we admit, but in any person only one 'feeler' of the real self is coming through; you do not know what the higher consciousness has stored within it.

When the soul has acquired all the lessons necessary; when it has attained a degree of completeness, it puts forth a more complete presentation of itself, and then you are able to see and recognize a master, an adept, an initiate. That soul is putting forth, not its entire self, even then, but the greater proportion, because it is ready to serve humanity in its own particular way. But do not think that the younger soul is giving its true nature. That remains in the higher consciousness.

You know, it does not matter very much who is a great soul and who is a young soul. We do not think it matters at all. Do not worship one who you think is great, but endeavour to love all, both great and small, young and old. Love them all. All are the same in God's sight.

Is it possible to remain aware of the higher consciousness which you have, all through the working day? It is possible, but difficult. It comes with continual aspiration and self-discipline. As you progress on the path of continual meditation, you get two levels of consciousness—that is to say, you may be engaged in everyday things on the surface, but beneath the surface there is always this consciousness of the universal divine love. You become aware beneath the daily consciousness all the time.

A time will come, though, when every soul will be aware of its higher life and of its true self. Then it will be able to see the two selves in contrast—the limited earthly self and the higher, heavenly and eternal self. As development proceeds, the higher self becomes stronger and more in evidence in everyday life. Then problems and difficulties no longer overwhelm the soul; they keep to their rightful place. The soul develops vision, not only of God and of heavenly things, but also of earthly things. It sees things in their true perspective, and its sensitivity enables it to penetrate the ethers and to receive radiation from the higher worlds.

To achieve what we have told you you can find, you must work steadily onward. And we tell you that if you can put into practice in your daily life one iota of what you hear or read, flowing through from us in words, you will do very well indeed!

When a measure of control has been earned, when these earthly tests have been safely passed, the time always comes for a person to be summoned into the great Hall of Initiation. The soul is led by the guide through many intricate ways, many dark passages— which is what you are going through now in your earthly life. You do not know where your road leads, nor when you will turn the corner, nor what you will find round it. Human life is really a passage through which the being—man or woman—is being led by its guide, not only in one incarnation, but through many.

At long last the soul comes into some gracious and beautiful place, and is led up to the blazing altar of light—so strong that it may be that the eyes must be veiled. But at the end of the great ceremony the eyes are no longer blindfolded. They behold the blazing Star, the Star of six points; six outer points, but with one central point, seven points in all. This seven-pointed Star corresponds to the seven great rays of life, the seven rays which come from the seven angels round the throne of God. Through a long, long journey each soul has also been learning, training, gaining power to

The Best of White Eagle

156

send forth the light from every one of the seven sacred centres in its own body, and to draw upon the seven sacred planetary forces which work through each sign of the zodiac. Perfected man–woman not only sees that blazing Star at his or her initiation, but realizes that he or she in truth *is* that Star.

The Wise Knight

EVERY soul at some time must make its stand for truth, must stand forth as a warrior, and fight for what it knows to be right and true. Sometimes it may have been described to you, or seen in your meditations: a knight in shining armour, holding aloft the sword of truth. This shining knight symbolizes your higher self, or your guide. This guide of your soul may come to you clothed in many different ways. He or she may adopt the astral body of any one of his or her previous incarnations or may wear the garment of pure spirit—shall we call it the heavenly raiment of flashing light and beauty? If you will visualize your guide in this way, you will attune yourself to the planes of pure spirit, and to do this must be your object each day if you would tread the way of the disciple.

It is a common error in early stages on the spiritual path to daydream, to live in a remote and nebulous state, sometimes of self-glorification, sometimes of an unbalanced emotionalism like that of a young pupil for an adored teacher. But the disciple on the path cannot live in this nebulous, dreamy state; the student must come to grips with the problems of everyday life and human relationships in a practical and loving way. The very best school for the pupil-disciple is that of everyday contacts with ordinary people in an everyday world. The friction of daily life is the process which smoothes off the surfaces of the 'rough ashlar' of the apprentice so that it becomes the perfect cube of the master Mason.

No one can run away from their life-experience. We say this with great earnestness. However often you run away from your lessons, again and again and again you will be faced with the same cycle of experience until some weakness or defect is at last erased, some lesson learned.

God, the supreme light and glory of life, is all-wise, and God's nature is love; all creation is subject to the law of love. Therefore we should welcome those very circumstances against which our lower nature and our lower self rebels, and be brave warriors in the field of battle, knowing that the end is love.

The Example You Set

BEAUTIFUL ROAD HOME

BE STILL. Keep very still and quiet within. Ask, and God or your guardian angel will help you. Maybe you won't understand that you are being helped by someone *outside* yourself, but it will work. So, be still inside. Keep very calm and let the power of God assist you as it will....

Some of you have to face sickness and presently old age; some have to face frustration, or endure very hard work, or suffer disappointment; most of you feel that you are carrying a heavy burden. Are you meant to throw your burdens away and become

The Best of White Eagle

careless? No, but you have to recognize the value of all these things, and to see beyond them. Pray to see what these burdens can teach you. Sometimes the question arises, 'What am I to do? Am I to do this or that? Do I stay, go here or go there?'. Our answer to such questions is this: do the job which God has placed immediately before you. Have you ever thought that your work has been placed before you by God in order to give you an opportunity to develop your character, your spiritual sensitivity and gifts, and also as an opportunity to help others too by your example? We wonder sometimes how many of our brethren remember this point—the example that they are setting in the world?

Before you all opens a path of light that is leading you onward and upward to attain someday to indescribable happiness and satisfaction, because you will have fulfilled the real purpose of life. When men and women fulfil this purpose, they are filled with peace and happiness. We know, we know, about your present-day sorrows and the problems that you must face. We know how you feel. We too can feel exactly the same because we feel *through you*, we feel *with you;* but always we know that this heavenly power is working, working, working through all the affairs of the individual, slowly to bring about illumination of their soul and their eventual happiness.

Never look back with regret; that is a waste of time. Do your best honourably. Let that inner voice speak, whatever the circumstances in which you are placed. Be careful what you say, because the tongue can hurt others and it can make much mischief. So be careful what you say. Always speak the truth.

Truth

*T*HE SOUL *setting forth on the spiritual path can become absorbed in its own progress, or become inflated with its own spiritual grandeur and power. But if the soul has striven with all its might to follow in the footsteps of Christ; if the soul has endeavoured truly to absorb the gentle humility of the Christ, it can never lose itself in self-glorification, for then it knows that it is neither great nor wonderful, that of itself it could not heal, teach or give comfort. The soul knows that any good flowing through it is of the Christ, is of God. The test, dear ones, is that of the Christ spirit; and if you can truly feel that the gentle, humble spirit of the Son of God is walking by your side, your hand in his, you cannot fail.*

JESUS TEACHER AND HEALER

*K*EEP *your feet on the earth but lift your face towards the heavens, for the light which floods into you from on high will steady your feet and guide them in the right path. Have confidence in this divine light. Surrender with a tranquil mind and a heart full of love to this infinite wisdom.*

THE QUIET MIND